GOD'S MESSAGE TO MEN

Strengthen Your Relationship with God,
Your Spouse, Your Children and Your World

Joseph Giammarco

Copyright © 2023 Joseph Giammarco
All rights reserved
First Edition

NEWMAN SPRINGS PUBLISHING
320 Broad Street
Red Bank, NJ 07701

First originally published by Newman Springs Publishing 2023

ISBN 978-1-68498-892-1 (Paperback)
ISBN 978-1-68498-893-8 (Digital)

Printed in the United States of America

DEDICATION

I wish to dedicate this book first and foremost to God who led me through this journey so far. Randall Wood, who led the trip to Ukraine and who gave me a chance to make materials what now is a book. Mark Arnold, who invited me to the Men of Standard Bible study that further transformed the original and who encouraged me to keep going. Similarly, Michael Martin, who hosted the twelve weeks in his home and, like Mark, constantly encouraged me. The Men of Standard, who then and still now pray for me through good times and bad. Finally, Brett Bohl, who through Faith in the Fairways, allowed me to write this book.

CONTENTS

Preface..vii

SECTION 1
FIRST PRIORITY IS GOD

Chapter 1: The Two-Foot Putt...1
Chapter 2: Back to the Future...6
Chapter 3: From Famous to Friend....................................14
Chapter 4: The Four Horsemen...21
Chapter 5: Campfire, Soap, Diamond, Flashlight,
 Owner's Manual, Romance Novel, Sharp
 Knife, Rudder, and Elephant Sandwich...........27
Chapter 6: The 5Ws and H of Prayer.................................34
Chapter 7: No Respect..43
Chapter 8: From Hundredth to First..................................51
Chapter 9: Paul, This Is Your Life.....................................61
Chapter 10: Top of the Leaderboard..................................72

SECTION 2
SECOND PRIORITY IS WIFE

Chapter 11: Cinderella...85
Chapter 12: Whole in One...90
Chapter 13: Angelo..100
Chapter 14: Love Your Wife...106

Chapter 15: Love Languages 114
Chapter 16: My Journey to Peace..116

Section 3
Third Priority Is Children

Chapter 17: Doughnut Holes 123
Chapter 18: Eyes of the Lord 125
Chapter 19: The Flying Wallendas...127
Chapter 20: Love Your Children 131
Chapter 21: Love Languages for Children................................137
Chapter 22: Ages and Stages 139
Chapter 23: Offensive Line..141
Chapter 24: Trash Van 143
Chapter 25: Not a Suggestion and Not Just for Kids.................146

Section 4
Fourth Priority Is World

Chapter 26: Mad Cow..151
Chapter 27: How Now Brown Cow...156
Chapter 28: Peace and Victory...164

PREFACE

This all started when I was forty-five years old. I asked God how can I glorify Him more when I retire. After much praying and pondering and a year passing, God gave me my first hint. While in Los Angeles on a business trip, I was listening to a Christian radio station. I don't remember the sermon, but I remember hearing a quiet voice say Ephesians 4:29, "Do not let any unwholesome talk come out of your mouths, but only what is helpful for building others up according to their needs, that it may benefit those who listen." This doesn't say much except I need to meet needs, but which ones and how. I continued to pray and ponder. At forty-six, God said to use how he shaped me. I had just heard a sermon about SHAPE. It's an acronym which means

S: Spiritual Gifts
H: Heart or Passion
A: Abilities
P: Personality
E: Experiences

Through this and Ephesians 4:29, God showed me, thru teaching, help men understand God better, strengthen Christian ministries and companies. What next, God? He told me to study the Bible in these areas. For two years, I did this, not knowing what this was leading to. Then at forty-eight years old, I saw in our church bulletin there was going to be a mission trip to Ukraine to encourage men, pastors, and Christian businesses. Wow, this is just what I was preparing for. I had only one problem. I only had less than one month to prepare three PowerPoint presentations from the pads of loose notes I had researched the last two years. I went to work, and it felt as if the Holy Spirit was moving my fingers. We went to Ukraine, and all the PowerPoint presentations were well received, especially the one to encourage men. When I came back, I asked God if this was it. About that time, a coworker and friend asked me where I've been. He hadn't seen me in a while. I told him I went on a mission trip and told him the three topics. He said they have been looking for someone to speak at his next Bible study. He asked me if I could do the one about men, but stretch it from one few hour session to twelve weeks. I finished the twelve weeks. By that time, I was forty-nine years old. After the Bible study group, I worked on a study to survey the congregation on how to strengthen the church. Next a friend had a ministry to the golf industry, Faith in the Fairway. The way it works on Tuesday evenings, he would have a special speaker give a sermon. He asked me if I wanted to participate; I said sure. I had to write out what was on PowerPoint since these were teleconferences. Little did I know, as my Bible study friends said, I'm writing a book. I did twelve Faith in the Fairway calls. I'm now fifty years old. The thirteenth Faith in the Fairway, I was going to do the purpose of marriage. I was stuck. I thouht this was important and I was struggling in my marriage too. By fifty-one, my wife had filed for divorce. By fifty-three, I was divorced. For the longest time, literally years, I didn't write a word. I felt no one would read a book like this by someone with a failed marriage. A lot of people encouraged me. So now at sixty-one and retired, I've written the book, including lessons I've learned from my own life. I hope you enjoy reading the book as much as I enjoyed writing it.

SECTION 1

FIRST PRIORITY IS GOD

CHAPTER 1

THE TWO-FOOT PUTT

The title of this first chapter is "The Two-Foot Putt." In golf, especially professional golf, when you get your ball two feet away from the hole, the pro rarely misses to get the ball in the hole. He still has to make it, but based on his or her skill, it's easy to get the ball in the hole. The reason I chose this title is in the Bible, there are four verses in the first chapter that sets the fundamental foundation for life. It's hard to miss! Like golfers who have several shots to get to the hole, there is plenty of opportunity to make mistakes. However, missing the two-foot putt should not happen. These verses should not be missed. These verses are the basic foundation of this book. These 2 out of all 31,103 verses or 0.006 percent are only a sliver of the entire Bible yet provides so much insight of how God wants us to live. Not only that it is in the first chapter of the Bible, so we get this insight right away. In fact, he creates the whole world and, right after that, tucks in these verses to help us understand how it all functions together. It's like getting a new car without an owner's manual. Certain things especially new technology features the user would have no idea how to use. Okay, let's jump right into these four verses. They are Genesis 1:27–28, "So God created mankind in his own image, in the image of God he created them; male and female he created them. God blessed them and said to them, 'Be fruitful and increase in number; fill the earth and subdue it. Rule over the fish in the sea and the birds in the sky and over every living creature that moves on the ground.'" Let's break these down further. "So God created mankind in his own image, in the image of God he created them."

This verse says not only that God created people, but they were the only part of creation he made like him. Also people were the only part of the creation God did not speak into existence. There is no "Let there be people!" In Genesis chapter 2, God further explains how He made Adam. Genesis 2:7 says "Then the Lord God formed a man from the dust of the ground and breathed into his nostrils the breath of life, and the man became a living being." This reminds me of my father, who had a 30 × 200 feet garden when he retired. Every spring, he would get on his hands and knees and shape the rows of dirt with his hands. For me, this was a tender memory of how much my father loved gardening.

It doesn't say, but I can imagine God getting on his hands and knees and lovingly shaping Adam and breathing life into his soil-formed lips. God stooped down and got His hands dirty to form man. For woman, he performed surgery. This picture also show how much God loves us. In Luke 12:6–7, it says, "Are not five sparrows sold for two pennies? Yet not one of them is forgotten by God. Indeed, the very hairs of your head are all numbered. Don't be afraid; you are worth more than many sparrows." Also in Psalm 139:13, it says, "For you created my inmost being; you knit me together in my mother's womb." You never hear about God counting leaves on a tree or knitting together in a cow's womb. Only with people. Even though all creation is special to God. He said it was all good. People are the crown jewel of his creation because he wants a special relationship with us. So in Genesis 1:27a, we learn the first and most important relationship is our relationship to God. The second part to Genesis 1:27a is Genesis 1:27b, "Male and female, he created them." So in Genesis 1:27b, we learn the second most important relationship is to our spouse. Moving on to Genesis 1:28, God blessed them and said to them, "Be fruitful and increase in number; fill the earth." So in Genesis 1:28a, we learn the third most important relationship is to our children. Finally, Genesis 1:28b says, "And subdue it. Rule over the fish in the sea and the birds in the sky and over every living creature that moves on the ground." So in Genesis 1:28b, we learn the fourth most important relationship is to our world. You may be thinking my marriage, children, and world are not a priority just God! I didn't say that. Every second of every day, these four relationships are jockeying for position. However, over all, God set four relationships in priority order. Relationship to God is first. See illustration below:

Fundamental Relationships

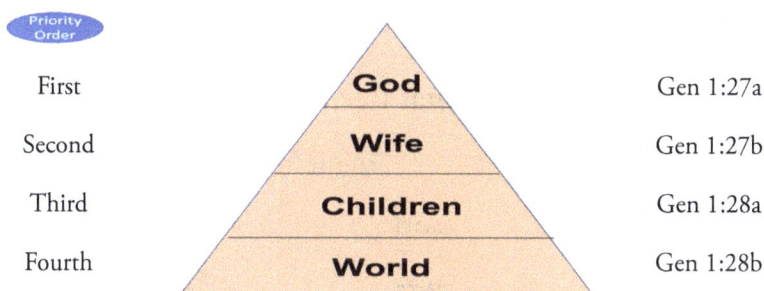

> God set four relationships in priority order.
> Relationship to God is first.

Further examining this relationship order, let's take a look at two verses. They are: Mark 8:36 which says, "What good is it for someone to gain the whole world, yet forfeit their soul?" Then Matthew 6:30–33 which says, "If that is how God clothes the grass of the field, which is here today and tomorrow is thrown into the fire, will he not much more clothe you—you of little faith? So do not worry, saying, 'What shall we eat?' or 'What shall we drink?' or 'What shall we wear?' For the pagans run after all these things, and your heavenly Father knows that you need them. But seek first his kingdom and his righteousness, and all these things will be given to you as well." Contrasting these two verses shows one is putting the world as a first priority leads to forfeiting your souls. Other translations say "leads to death." The second verse indicates putting God first will have the domino effect or by-product of providing all the other things you need. Sometimes, men especially focus on their careers first which is a part of the world relationship. Working backward from the previous illustration, being good in your career doesn't make you a good father, husband, or have a good relationship with God. However, having a good relationship with God has a positive influence on being a good husband, father, and manager of the world. Since one of God's goals is to make us like Jesus, would your wife, children, coworkers, neighbors notice anything different if you were more like Jesus. I bet so! Our second major point of this chapter is: focusing on relationship with God helps you have a strong relationship with wife, children, and world. See the illustration below.

Fundamental Relationships

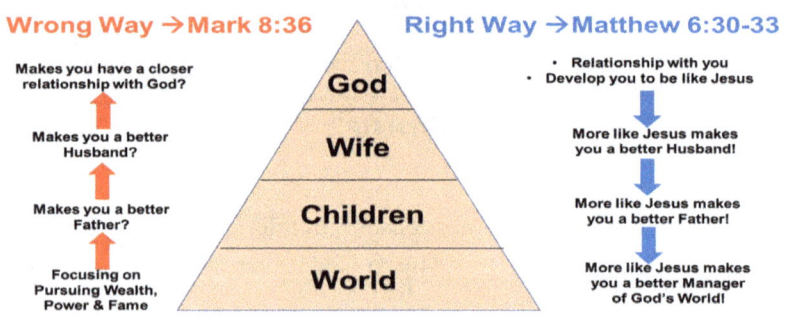

> Focusing on relationship with God helps you have a strong relationship with wife, children, and world.

You may be asking yourself, "Why are you focusing on me? Especially where I have to be a better husband, father, and worker. What if my wife, children, and coworkers don't cooperate?" As I said previously, the information in this book is good for everyone. However, I tailored it toward men since God assigned men as head of marriages and families, and as we'll read later, whether we like it or not, men are predominately in leadership positions in the world in places like government and industries. For all these reasons, God is counting on men to lead. So our final major point is: drawing closer to God draws you closer to families and world. Also, you draw families and world closer to God. The illustration below shows as you focus on God as your first priority relationship, you positively influence your other relationships.

Main Focus

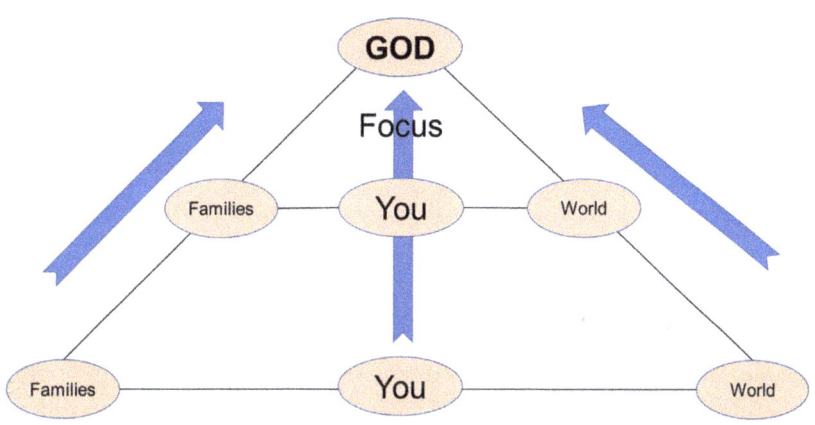

> Drawing closer to God draws you closer to families and world. Also, you draw families and world closer to God.

In summary, God set four relationships in priority order. Relationship to God is first. Don't miss this two-foot putt. In the next chapter, we will examine men in the Bible and how their relationships with God affected them, their families, society, and the future.

CHAPTER 2

BACK TO THE FUTURE

This next chapter is titled "Back to the Future" and is based on the popular movie. According to Wikipedia, *Back to the Future* is a 1985 American science fiction film. It stars Michael J. Fox and Christopher Lloyd. Set in 1985, the story follows Marty McFly (Fox), a teenager accidentally sent back to 1955 in a time-traveling DeLorean automobile built by his eccentric scientist friend Doctor Emmett "Doc" Brown (Lloyd). Trapped in the past, Marty inadvertently prevents his future parents' meeting—threatening his very existence—and is forced to reconcile the pair and somehow get back to the future. *Back to the Future* earned a worldwide gross of $381.1 million, making it the highest grossing film of 1985. I named this chapter "Back to the Future" because we are going to study men in the Bible, their relationship with God, and how it affected their lives, their family, their society and future generations. We're going to examine these areas in the life of Noah, Abraham, Moses, David, Korah, Ahab, and Haman. I'm going to list the Bible verses that apply to the particular man, and I recommend you read each of them. Because of space, I will only list them.

I'll give a short summary of each situation.

Noah Builds the Ark
Genesis 6:1–9:17

People had become so wicked God decides to destroy all people by flood. Noah was the only person who had a relationship with God, and it was positive. God asked Noah to build an Ark. The dimensions in feet of 450 long × 75 wide × 45 tall, which compares with 850 long × 92 wide × 64 tall for the *Titanic*. About 30 percent of the volume Ark compared to the Titanic. It took 1 man 100 years to build the Ark, whereas it took 14,000 men 3 years to build the Titanic. Also, the 14,000 men could concentrate where as people would stop by all the time to laugh at and ridicule the man building a big boat where there was no water in sight. I can imagine him telling them of the impending doom when the rain starts. They would laugh more since there had never been this thing called rain. Day after day for one hundred years, Noah faithfully followed God's plan. Then God told Noah to gather his family and two of every kind of animal and went into the ark and God shut the door. Just as God said, it rained for forty days and nights. Except for those on the ark, everything drowned. The rain stopped and the water receded, and Noah and his family and the animals in the ark repopulated the earth. We're here today because of Noah's faithfulness to God.

Abraham Promised a Future Nation
Genesis 12:1–9, 15:1–20, 17:1–8, 21:1–7, and 22:1–18

Abraham was seventy-five years old when God revealed Himself to him. Abraham was living in Ur, which is now modern-day Iraq. God told Abraham to leave Ur and go to Canaan, which is now modern-day Israel, where he would make his descendants into a great nation, and from the nation would come someone who would bless the entire world. Abraham had no children and his wife Sarah was sixty-five and barren. This trip was no hop, skip, and a jump. It is estimated to have been 3,461 miles. Compare this to the distance from NYC to LA is 2,790 miles. Obviously a long trip, 1.24 times the trip from NYC to LA. The method of travel, walking or riding an animal versus car, and dirt paths versus paved roads. I can imagine when Abraham told his wife, relatives, and friends what he was going to do and why they probably thought he was crazy. Nonetheless, Abraham obeyed God. Over the next twenty-five years, God continues to reinforce the promises of the birth of a son. Then Abraham, at the age of one hundred, and Sarah, at age ninety, had a son and named him Isaac. Finally, a son whose heirs would inherit the land and it would become Israel (Isaac's son Jacob God renamed Israel). But wait, God asked Abraham to sacrifice (kill) Isaac when he was a child. Well then, how was a nation formed if Isaac is dead? When Abraham was about to do it, God stopped him. God commended Abraham for his faith and obedience. All was well, and God's plan for the nation of Israel to exist and from this nation came Jesus who would bless the world!

Moses and the Golden Calves
Exodus 32:1–35

While Moses was up on the mountain receiving the Ten Commandments, the second one being "Do not make any idols," the people became impatient because Moses stayed up longer than expected, so they went to Aaron (Moses's brother and Chief Priest) and said, "We don't know where Moses has gone so make us golden calves and they will be our gods." Aaron caved in and agreed. He asked all the people to give gold for making the idols. After they finished, they held a big celebration and partied their socks off. Right about then, Moses came down. God was so mad, he told Moses to leave him alone so he can destroy all the people. God had had it with the people since this was not the first time they disobeyed. There have been several. God was going to destroy two million people and start over a new nation starting with Moses. However, Moses pleaded with God. Moses reminded God what would Pharaoh think when he heard God killed all the people he delivered from Pharaoh. Also, what about God's promise to Abraham, Isaac, and Jacob (Israel) about creating a nation? Finally, Moses told God to punish him only and spare the people. God listened to Moses and relented from His anger and spared the people. Had Moses not done that, two million people would have perished and probably the nation of Israel would not exist and maybe Jesus would not come to bless the whole world. God's respect for Moses and Moses's faith in God's love prevented all these things from happening.

David Rescues His Family
1 Samuel 30:1–31

At this time, even though David was anointed king instead of Saul, he was on the run from King Saul. King Saul so intensely hunted David that David decided to move to the Philistine country and pretend to ally with them. He convinced the Philistine king he was loyal. However, the Philistine generals were leery that in a battle with Israel, David would turn on them. So the Philistine king asked David and his men to sit out the impending battle with Israel. When David and his men returned home, they found the city burned and all the wives, children, and possessions taken. David's men were so distraught, they wanted to stone him to death. David prayed to God whether to pursue the raiders or not. God told David he would be successful. So David pursued the raiders and came across an injured slave left behind by the raiders who helped David find the raider's location. David and his men recovered their wives, children, and possessions. Instead of stoning David, they cheered him as a hero. All because David trusted in God

David Promised Eternal Blessings
2 Samuel 7:1–17

David fought in many battles as king. Eventually, things calmed down and David became preoccupied with fact that he lived in a palace while Israelites came to worship and sacrifice to God in a tent. How embarrassing! David started to make plans to build a temple in Jerusalem to replace the tent. God sent a messenger to David to say, "Don't worry because I created the world and am everywhere all the time. I want you to leave the building of the temple to your son Solomon who will be king after you. What I really want you to know, King David, is because you have followed and trusted me, I promise there will always be one of your decedents on the throne of Israel." What a nice promise! But wait! After King Solomon, the kingdom split, and David's descendants controlled only two of the twelve tribes. The two tribes became known as Judah. Then later, other nations like Babylon, Persia, and Rome conquered the land and removed the kings. Even today, Israel is led by a prime minister (like a president) and there is no king. So what about this promise? It seems very shallow. But wait! Jesus is a descendant of King David, and He sits on the throne in heaven for all eternity as King of kings and Lord of lords. All this because David was a man after God's own heart.

Korah Challenges Moses's leadership
Numbers 16:1–50

Korah was a descendant of Levi, so he was a priest in Israel. He, Dathan, and Abiram complained Moses and Aaron, whom God picked to lead the people, especially Moses had too much power and had led long enough. Korah and the others wanted to take over and lead the people. When Moses heard about it, he fell on his face before the Lord. He told Korah and his followers to stand at the openings of their tents with incense, and if they died a natural death, then God did not choose Moses and Aaron, but if they died some unusual way, then God chose Moses and Aaron. Suddenly, the earth opened and swallowed up the tents of Korah, Dathan, and Abiram along with their wives, children, and all their possessions. They had 250 other men with incense and fire came down from the sky and burned them up. For further punishment, God started a plague. Moses recognized it and told Aaron to immediately go among the people with his incense, which stopped the plague. However, the plague killed 14,700 people. All this because Korah challenged God's Authority.

Ahab: God Destroys His Family
1 Kings 22:10–40 and 2 Kings 9:7–37

King Ahab and Queen Jezebel were the most wicked king and queen of Judah and Israel combined. Not only did they worship a false god (Baal), but they caused the nation to abandon God and worship Baal. Judah and Israel were at war with Syria at that time and Ahab and the king of Israel called together all their prophets to ask them whether God thinks they should attack. They all said to attack and be victorious. Ahab knew one of the prophets and didn't like him, but asked him whether they should attack. He said the same as the others. Then Ahab said to tell him the truth. The prophet said there was a meeting in heaven how to lure Ahab to his death. The idea came to put a lying spirit in all the prophets who would say they should attack and be successful. Ahab ignored the prophet and went ahead to fight the Syrians. He was killed in battle. The king of Israel was wounded, but not killed. Later another prophet (Elisha) anointed Jehu as king of Israel. He killed the wounded king of Israel, Ahab's son, the new king of Judah, and had Jezebel thrown out the window where she died. The dogs ate her and licked her blood and there was nothing left except her head, hands, and feet. Ahab had seventy sons. Jehu killed them too. Ahab and Jezebel's entire family was wiped out. All because they would not worship God.

Haman Plots against the Jews
Esther 5:9–9:32

When the Medes and Persians had control over Israel and Judah, they took people into captivity. Two of those where Esther who became queen and Mordecai who worked in the palace and was related to Esther. Haman, a prince in the king's court and later became the chief prince and everyone bowed down to him except Mordecai. He would only bow down to God. That made Haman mad, so he decided he was going to wipe out all the Jews (he didn't know Queen Esther was a Jew). He convinced the king the Jews were causing trouble and to agree to a nonrevokable law that on a certain date, everyone should attack the Jews, kill them, and take all their possessions. When Mordecai found out, he urged her to tell the king. She had to be careful because if she approached the king without his permission, she could be killed. She asked Mordecai to pray for her as she approached the king and Haman together. She told the king she was a Jew and of Haman's plot to eliminate the Jews. The king was furious and had Haman and his ten sons hung on the gallows he had made for Mordecai. Mordecai was elevated to Haman's position, and they made another law that on the same date as the other, the Jews could fight back. As a result, everyone was afraid of the Jews and did not attack.

Next, we'll summarize these eight cases and see how they effected the man, his family, society, and future generations. The first five, the men had a positive relationship with God, and the last three, they didn't. The next page is a table with the summary.

Study of Men in the Bible

Who	+/- Relation with God	Effect on Man	Effect on Family	Effect on Society/ Future Generations
Noah Builds the Ark	+	Noah's life saved. Learned trust and obedience.	Lives were saved.	World preserved. People can have a relationship with God thru Jesus.
Abraham Promised a Future Nation	+	Learned to have faith and trust in God.	Isaac was born.	The Israelite nation was formed, and Jesus was born out of this nation and blessed the whole world. People can have a relationship with God thru Jesus.
Moses and the Golden Calves	+	Was able to persuade God not to wipe out the Israelites.	As part of the Israelite nation, they were saved.	Israelite nation was not wiped out, and Jesus was born out of this nation and blessed the whole world. People can have a relationship with God thru Jesus.

Who	+/- Relation with God	Effect on Man	Effect on Man	Effect on Society/ Future Generations
David Rescues His Family	+	David was a hero and not stoned to death. Learned to trust in God.	Rescued.	All the families' lives and possessions returned. See an example of trusting God.
David Promised Eternal Blessings	+	David learned to have faith and trust in God.	Solomon built the temple.	Jesus would sit on the throne in heaven forever. People can have a relationship with God thru Jesus.
Korah Challenges Moses's Leadership	-	Korah, Dathan, and Abiram killed.	Families killed.	About 15,000 Israelites died that day. Korah, Dathan, and Abiram family line wiped out. Confidence in Moses as leader.
Ahab: God Destroys His Family	-	Ahab killed in battle with the Syrians.	Jezebel and all of Ahab's sons killed by Jehu.	Ahab family line wiped out. People returned to worshiping God.
Haman Plots against the Jews	-	Haman hung on the gallows he built to hang Mordecai.	Ten sons hung on the same gallows.	Jews saved. People feared the Jews. Haman family line wiped out.

In looking at the summary, it's clear that having positive relationship positively impacts the man, his family, his society, and the future generations. The reverse is true for a negative relationship. Also, we see that God had a plan to deal with the problem of disobedience or sin though creating a nation where someone would come to bless the whole world (Jesus). Anyone getting in the way of that plan better watch out! In the next chapter, we'll talk more about this plan. In conclusion, we can say your relationship to others is affected by your relationship to God. Focus on your relationship to God.

CHAPTER 3

From Famous to Friend

Just a quick recap, in "The Two-Foot Putt," we learned God created four relationships for us: first a relationship with God, second with our spouse, third with our children, and fourth with our world. He put them in priority order with God being first. Then in the last chapter, "Back to the Future," we talked about how our positive relationship with God not only benefits us, but as a by-product, positively affects our other relationships now and in the future and even beyond our lives here on earth. Continuing yet further in the first two chapters, we learned how beneficial and important to have a personal relationship with God. I hope you're excited as I am about having a personal relationship with God. This chapter is titled "From Famous to Friend." When I was growing up, I started playing golf around the time Jack Nicklaus was in his prime in the PGA Tour (as of this writing, he is considered the greatest golfer of all time). I would watch him play on TV often. I especially liked him because he was from my hometown (Columbus, Ohio) and went to the Ohio State University as I did. I can even remember when I was in high school going to the first Memorial Tournament played on a course Jack designed. For many years now, the Memorial Tournament is a regular stop on the PGA Tour, and the best golfers come to play each year. I saw Jack and Lee Trevino. I was probably only twenty feet away and heard him speak and watched him play. Years later, I moved down the road from the Muirfield Village Golf Course where the tournament is played each year. There is a statue of Jack near the entrance to the golf course where he's showing a boy how to play golf. I often pass by this statue driving to and from home, and it brings up fond memories I have of Jack Nicklaus. I hope you can see I'm very interested in Jack Nicklaus. He is famous to me! However, he's not my friend. As much as I know about his fame, I think it would be greater to be his friend and have a personal relationship with him. This is the same with God. He's famous to us. We're familiar with all he's done. How he created the world, delivered the Israelites from Pharaoh, and so much more. We may have even visited his house, the church; heard him speak through his word, the Bible; and even know people who know him like our parents and friends. He's certainly famous to us, but can we call him our friend? Someone we have a personal relationship with? Not necessarily. Is this automatic? Are we born having this relationship? Did we inherit it from our parents? Do we have to work for it or pay for it somehow? In the rest of this chapter, I'd like to answer the question how to start a personal relationship with God? Well, first, like any relationship, it begins with two people with something in common. Let's look at God's characteristics and ours as well. He is the Creator, and we are His beloved creation made in his image, and He wants to have a personal relationship with us. He's all knowing, ever present, all powerful, and perfectly good. He has rules and expects them to be obeyed, and us having the free will to obey those rules or not. You see perfect Holy God doesn't mix well with people who choose to disobey his rules. It's as if Jack said to me, "It's great we have a lot in common, but if you want to be my friend, you have to play golf as good as I do." I would be absolutely stuck!

Maybe some of you could do that, but I would be absolutely stuck! Now let's look at some verses from the Bible. In John 3:16, Jesus said, "God so loved the world that he gave his one and only Son, that whoever believes in him shall not perish but have eternal life." This verse is probably the most famous. You may remember seeing this verse flash at NFL games with a man with a rainbow-colored afro, and since then, you may have seen it at other events and maybe golf events as well. This verse says it all. It says:

1. God loves us and wants a relationship with us.
2. For some reason, we are perishing
3. God sent Jesus to make a way to rescue us and to be reunited with God.

I won't elaborate a lot about God loving us and wanting a relationship with us. I think that's pretty well understood. Let's talk about the part where we are perishing. Why is that? Why would we be perishing? We read in Romans 3:23, "For all have sinned and fall short of the glory of God," and in Romans 6:23, it says, "For the wages of sin is death, but the gift of God is eternal life in Christ Jesus our Lord." This teaches us that our problem in having a true relationship with God is sin. We've all disobeyed God, and as a consequence, we are separated from Him here on earth and in eternity. The last part of Romans 6:23 talks about God giving us a gift of eternal life. Well, if we've broken God's rules and are separated from Him, why would he give us a gift? Why would we need Jesus? Why couldn't we solve the sin problem ourselves? We read in Ephesians 2:8–9, "For it is by grace you have been saved, through faith—and this is not from yourselves, it is the gift of God—not by works, so that no one can boast." So we can't solve the sin problem ourselves. God has to provide the solution for us and give it to us as a gift. Back to Jack Nicklaus, if I tried very hard, as hard as I could, I could never play as good as Jack. He would need to give a gift to me, so I could meet his standard. Interestingly, most world religions believe God and people are in conflict somehow over sin. However, for those religions, the solution is through working hard to have their good deeds outweigh their sins. There is not an exact formula when this is exactly achieved, and we're never quite sure when we've done achieving it. Only in the God of the Bible does he provide the way to solve the sin problem. The word *grace* is used often to describe it. The acrostic is God's Riches at Christ's Expense. This gift we don't deserve, but God gives it to us anyways. Let's look at a few more verses. First John 1:9, "If we confess our sins, he is faithful and just and will forgive us our sins and purify us from all unrighteousness." God tells us the first step is to recognize that we have disobeyed him and he will forgive us. However, that's not all. God says the penalty for sin is separation and death. Even though he loves us and wants to forgive us, he still has to punish sin. Sometimes, we think of God as a grandfather who comes to visit and lets us do all the things that our parents don't allow and then doesn't correct us for it as well. God is actually more like a parent who loves us and disciplines us when we disobey. Maybe that's why they call him God the Father and not God the Grandfather. This poses a great catch-22. We know we've sinned, but I mentioned earlier we cannot escape the punishment we deserve. During Old Testament times, God introduced to the Israelites the concept of animal sacrifice. God told them if they sinned, to bring one of their animals like a sheep to the temple. The animal was not to have a defect. In other words, they couldn't just bring to God what they didn't value themselves. They would place the animal on the altar and place their hands on its head, symbolizing the animal taking on the sin of the person. They would kill the animal, thus paying for the sin. The animal was a substitute for them. Jesus said in John 3:16, "God so loved the world that he gave his one and only Son, that whoever believes in him shall not perish but have eternal life." To finally put the issue to rest, God Himself became the perfect sinless lamb and took upon himself our sins and paid the penalty of a brutal death on the cross as a substitute for us. Once and for all, Jesus provided for us a way to escape the judgement of sin. Jesus said in John 14:6, "I am the way and the truth and the life. No one comes to the Father except through me." This tells us that we have a way to have a relationship with God. In the case of our Jack Nicklaus story, to be his friend, we have to play as good as him. He could give us Arnold Palmer riding in the cart and play best ball. We would always use his shots which would fulfill the requirement. Pretty neat that God provides a way of salvation. It says in Romans 10:9, "If you declare with your mouth, 'Jesus is Lord,' and believe in your heart that God raised him from the dead, you will be saved." Since he not only died but is alive again, we know his words are trustworthy and true. Believing Jesus guarantees salvation. Even though the animal in the Old Testament fulfilled the role of the substitute, the person still had to believe and choose to accept this way of atonement. In the story about Jack, we still had to believe Jack's telling the truth and Arnold has the ability to play great golf and, based on those two things, accept his offer. Jesus said in Revelation 3:20, "Here I am! I stand at the door and knock. If anyone hears my voice and opens the door, I will come in and eat with that person, and they with me." Finally, just because we go to church or read the Bible or pray or do good deeds doesn't give us a personal relationship with God. Only through an act of accepting Jesus as Lord and Savior does. As the last verse we read says Jesus wants this for us. He is knocking and inviting us to answer, but we have the invitation. It's as simple as ABC.

    A: Admit you have sinned.
    B: Believe Jesus has the power to save you.
    C: Confess or accept Jesus as Lord and Savior.

In the illustration, there is God in heaven and us on the earth, and we are separated by a great chasm. The great chasm represents sin. Jesus came from heaven to earth, died on a cross, rose again, and returned to heaven. He placed the cross across the chasm as a bridge between God and people. Each one of us is given a choice between eternal relationship with God or eternal separation from God.

Step 1
Starting a Relationship with God

> Jesus spoke these words, "God so loved the world that he gave his one and only Son that whoever believes in him shall not perish but have eternal life" (John 3:16).

God's Invitation:
1) God loves you.
2) Your sin separates you from God.
3) Jesus paid the penalty of sin by dying on the cross and rising to life.
4) God wants to forgive you if you are willing to ask for forgiveness and accept Jesus as Lord and Savior.
5) Through sincere prayer, accept God's offer now!

As I was preparing this chapter, it dawned on me that it's harder to have a relationship with Jack Nicklaus than with God. Isn't that incredible! When I was eighteen, a college classmate explained this message to me and this message is called the Gospel or Good News. Frankly, I thought he was kind of weird, and this message was a little strange. However, over time, I began to realize the message was really good news. And at that point, I accepted Jesus as my Lord and Savior, and that's when I started my personal relationship with God. That was over forty years ago, and it's made an incredible difference in my life. However, you know what? I still don't know Jack Nicklaus as a friend! Maybe someday, one of you will introduce me to him. Until then, he's only famous to me. But as for God, he's not only famous but my friend as well. I hope you can say He's your friend too and you can say when you started your personal relationship with God. If you haven't made that decision yet, it's not too late. God accepts you as you are. If you want to start a personal relationship with God, simply pray to God in your own words these three things:

1. Admit to God you you've sinned and you want his forgiveness.
2. Realize there is nothing you can do to pay for those sins yourself, and you accept what Jesus did on the Cross as Savior to pay for your sins.
3. Thank Jesus and ask Him to take hold of your life and be your Lord and make you all He created you to be.

If you sincerely pray that prayer, that simple prayer God promises to forgive you and you can live with God in eternity.

Next Step: Reflection, Application, and Action

Not at all (0) — Slightly (2) — Some (4) — Much (6) — Very Much (8) — Perfect =Jesus (10)

Ask God to reveal where you are, what to do next, and to help you (five or below should take action).

Priority	Basic Question	Statement	Rating	Action to Improve	New Rating	Difference in Rating
First: God	Do I have a relationship with God?	I've started a relationship with God through accepting Jesus as Lord and Savior				

CHAPTER 4

The Four Horsemen

As I shared, I've been building a message from God to us. The first time we learned God created us to have four types of relationships. They are: first a relationship with Him, second with our spouse, third with our children, and fourth with our world. He put them in priority order with God being first. Then we learned our relationship with God not only benefits us, but as a by-product, positively affects our other relationships now and in the future, even beyond our lives here on earth. Next, we learned we can start a personal relationship with God by simply asking for forgiveness and accepting Jesus as Lord and Savior. And last time, we learned that once we begin our relationship with God, things don't stop there, but that is just the beginning. God wants to develop us to have a character like Jesus. I'd like to continue building on what we learned so far. This chapter is titled "The Four Horsemen." The Four Horsemen I'm talking about are the Four Horsemen of Notre Dame who were the backfield of Notre Dame's 1924 football team under Coach Knute Rockne. To achieve football immortality after Notre Dame's 13–7 upset victory over a strong army team, sportswriter

Grantland Rice of the *New York Herald* penned a famous passage of sports journalism. He wrote:

> Outlined against a blue-gray October sky, the Four Horsemen rode again. In dramatic lore their names are Death, Destruction, Pestilence, and Famine. But those are aliases. Their real names are: Stuhldreher, Crowley, Miller, and Layden. They formed the crest of the South Bend cyclone before which another fighting Army team was swept over the precipice at the Polo Grounds this afternoon as 55,000 spectators peered down upon the bewildering panorama spread out upon the green plain below. After that win over Army, the Irish were rarely threatened the rest of the year. A 27–10 win over Stanford in the 1925 Rose Bowl gave Rockne and Notre Dame the national championship and a perfect 10–0 record. Although none of the four stood taller than six feet and none of the four weighed more than 162 pounds, the Four Horsemen might comprise the greatest backfield ever. As a unit, they played 30 games and only lost two games. They played at a time when there were no separate offensive and defensive teams. All players had to play both sides. Once a player left the field, he could not come back into the game. All four players were elected to the College Football Hall of Fame. Interestingly, after graduation, the lives of the Four Horsemen took similar paths. All began coaching careers.

In preparation for this message, I watched the movie *Knute Rockne All American*, starring Pat O'Brien as Knute Rockne. In the movie, there is a scene where Coach Rockne rewards his team for a great win by taking them to see a show with chorus girls; while there, he was inspired by the synchronized dancing. While his players gawk at the pretty girls, Rockne takes notes and draws out the new backfield shift. He returns home where his wife and two university professors are waiting for him. He says to them, "I saw something tonight. Got the idea of a lifetime…of a lifetime! Professor, Doc, I saw a show tonight in Chicago…chorus girls, a whole row of them… what rhythm, it was like poetry just watching them move…beautiful, effortless…effortless! Get the idea. They gave me the idea for a new kind of backfield shift…and, gentlemen, it will revolutionize the game. Revolutionize it! No lost motion, no wasted momentum, split-second timing. I can see it now…the public…the public will love it! It's new, it's colorful, and it's got great showmanship…and it's new! It's new!"

Next, we see the four players in what looks like a dance studio trying the backfield shift to the same music as the chorus girls danced to. They struggle to attempt the backfield shift and seem to have all left feet. Rockne continues to push and drill them. He says to them, "Okay, come on, boys…let's get smart. You can get this shift, I know you can…that's why I selected you to do it. Of course I know it's tricky, but that's the beauty of it. If you get it, it will revolutionize football!"

Next we see them on the gridiron after undoubtedly much practice, but this time, instead of four clumsy players, they are a well-oiled unit executing the backfield shift flawlessly. Using this new backfield shift, they terrorize all teams. The narrator says, "What is this new miracle that Knute Rockne has wrought?"

This bolt of Irish Lightning that strikes from all sides with such blinding speed and fury. A shift they call it. Yes, but Heisman of Georgia Tech also has a shift. So has Thad Jones of Yale. But theirs are simple tunes compared to Rockne's symphony. For this shift is music. The music of a master's hand. Knute Rockne whose ingenious brain has perfected the pass has brought a great new thrill to football and to its millions of followers. Well, what does this have to do with God? Well, God has His own Four Horsemen. He provides them for us and uses them to develop us. They are the Bible, Prayer, the Holy Spirit, and the Church. And just like the Notre Dame

Four Horsemen who all went into coaching, God's Four Horsemen coach us. And just like the Notre Dame Four Horsemen who worked together and synchronized as a unit, God's Four Horsemen work together to develop and transform us into the character of Jesus as well as strengthen our relationship with God. Let's talk about each one briefly.

The Bible: In John 1:1, it says, "In the beginning was the Word, and the Word was with God, and the Word was God." And later in John 1:14, it says, "The Word became flesh and made his dwelling among us." We have seen his glory, the glory of the one and only Son, who came from the Father, full of grace and truth. Whenever I read that passage of scripture, chills run up and down my spine. It reminds me that God came down to us, and whenever I read any scripture, I'm literally hearing Jesus like the disciples did as they sat at His feet. Sometimes, we get frustrated because we don't hear God or we want to know how to hear God. By reading and meditating on God's Word, we hear God. Just like any friend, we have to have communication. Thru the Bible, God talks to us.

Prayer: Jesus said in Matthew 7:7–11, "Ask and it will be given to you; seek and you will find; knock and the door will be opened to you. For everyone who asks receives; the one who seeks finds; and to the one who knocks, the door will be opened. Which of you, if your son asks for bread, will give him a stone? Or if he asks for a fish, will give him a snake? If you, then, though you are evil, know how to give good gifts to your children, how much more will your Father in heaven give good gifts to those who ask him!" Prayer is how we talk to God. Thru the Bible and prayer, we have two-way communications with God and us. The 7:11 in Matthew 7:7–11 reminds me of the 7-Eleven convenient stores which was one of the first stores to be open seven days a week and twenty-four hours a day. We are able to communicate with God 24/7. He is always open to us. Communicating with God helps us to know Him better and for Him to help develop us. An easy way to remember prayer is the word ASK. This reminds us to Ask, Seek, and Knock.

Holy Spirit. When Jesus was about to ascend into heaven, his disciples undoubtedly didn't want Him to leave. He said to them in

John 16:5–13, "But now I am going to him who sent me. None of you asks me, 'Where are you going?' Rather, you are filled with grief because I have said these things. But very truly I tell you, it is for your good that I am going away. Unless I go away, the Advocate will not come to you; but if I go, I will send him to you. When he comes, he will prove the world to be in the wrong about sin and righteousness and judgment: about sin, because people do not believe in me; about righteousness, because I am going to the Father, where you can see me no longer; and about judgment, because the prince of this world now stands condemned. I have much more to say to you, more than you can now bear. But when he, the Spirit of truth, comes, he will guide you into all the truth. He will not speak on his own; he will speak only what he hears, and he will tell you what is yet to come." As humans, we are unable to fathom God. The Holy Spirit acts as a translator to help us understand God. Even though some person may have shared the Gospel, it was the Holy Spirit who revealed our need to accept Jesus as Lord and Savior and compels us to do it. Once we have a personal relationship with God, the Holy Spirit helps us understand, guides us, and gives us the power to carry out God's mission for us. When we don't study the Bible and pray, we hinder the ability of the Holy Spirit to reveal or interpret. In Ephesians 5:17–18, it says, "Therefore do not be foolish, but understand what the Lord's will is. Do not get drunk on wine, which leads to debauchery. Instead, be filled with the Spirit." One of the keys of being countinuosly filled by the Spirit is getting a steady diet of God's Word and keeping open communication with God. By doing this, we invite the Holy Spirit in and give Him lots of opportunity to impact our lives.

The Church: In Ephesians 5:22–27, it says, "Wives, submit yourselves to your own husbands as you do to the Lord. For the husband is the head of the wife as Christ is the head of the church, his body, of which he is the Savior. Now as the church submits to Christ, so also wives should submit to their husbands in everything. Husbands, love your wives, just as Christ loved the church and gave himself up for her to make her holy, cleansing[b] her by the washing with water through the word, and to present her to himself as a radiant church, without stain or wrinkle or any other blemish, but holy and blameless." Then in Revelation 19:6–8, it says, "Then I heard what sounded like a great multitude, like the roar of rushing waters and like loud peals of thunder, shouting: "Hallelujah! For our Lord God Almighty reigns. Let us rejoice and be glad and give him glory! For the wedding of the Lamb has come, and his bride has made herself ready. Fine linen, bright and clean, was given her to wear." (Fine linen stands for the righteous acts of God's holy people.) Obviously, these verses are great instruction for marriage. Also, they illustrate the relationship the church has to Jesus. The church is God's body here on earth which enjoys a special relationship to Jesus. The church is not just a physical building, but more importantly, a body of believers collectively worshipping God, maturing as disciples, encouraging and ministering to one another, and where we get mobilized to serve and tell others about Jesus. In the next chapters, I'd like to delve into each one of God's Four Horseman more deeply. However, this chapter's major point is to help you see how God has provided these four opportunities to help us grow in our relationship and to help develop us to be more like Jesus. Having one or two or even three in our lives is good, but having all four working together simultaneously is *great* and will revolutionize our lives! I want to encourage you to engage in a steady dose of each of these. I'm sure if you get creative all of God's Four Horsemen will make a huge impact in your life. And instead of bringing Death, Destruction, Pestilence, and Famine, which the Notre Dame Four Horsemen brought upon other football teams, God's Four Horsemen will bring you life, peace, joy, and blessing. As you develop, let His Four Horsemen revolutionize your life.

CHAPTER 5

Campfire, Soap, Diamond, Flashlight, Owner's Manual, Romance Novel, Sharp Knife, Rudder, and Elephant Sandwich

In the last chapter, we learned God has provided the Bible, prayer, Holy Spirt, and the church to help us grow. I'd like to continue building on what we've learned so far. This chapter is titled "Campfire, Soap, Diamond, Flashlight, Owner's Manual, Romance Novel, Sharp Knife, Rudder, and Elephant Sandwich." These nine things describe the Bible's importance in developing our relationship with God and for Him to develop us to be more like Jesus. It says in Psalm 1:1–3, "Blessed is the one who does not walk in step with the wicked or stand in the way that sinners take or sit in the company of mockers, but whose delight is in the law of the Lord, and who meditates on his law day and night. That person is like a tree planted by streams of water, which yields its fruit in season and whose leaf does not wither—whatever they do prospers." There's obviously cause and effect here. To love God, we have to obey Him. To obey Him, we need to know His word. To know His word, we have to study regularly and apply it. This makes perfect sense. However, there is a startling statistic I heard twenty years ago that still stands true today and dramatically changed me. While at a Men's Bible study one morning, my pastor told us that statistical research shows only about 10 percent of Americans have read the Bible all the way through even though there is an average of three Bibles per home. I was ashamed and embarrassed to know I was part of the majority. Even though I had been a believer for twenty years at that point, I had never read the Bible! God made this stick in my mind and showed me that although all what I was doing was good, hearing Him through his word would draw me closer to Him. I made a goal to read the Bible in a year. After I accomplished this, I thought I would try again even though I wondered if reading it again would be a benefit. After all, I'm not one to read the same book twice. It's been twenty years later, and I tried to read the Bible every year. I haven't always succeeded, but I haven't gotten tired of it. Now I'd like to share what the Bible means to me and why I keep reading it.

Campfire: I enjoy camping and my favorite part is the evening campfire. You can relax, laugh, and talk. It says in John 1:1, "In the beginning was the Word, and the Word was with God, and the Word was God." Later, it says in John 1:14, "The Word became flesh and made his dwelling among us. We have seen his glory, the glory of the one and only Son, who came from the Father, full of grace and truth." Whenever I read these verses, it reminds me when I read scripture, I'm literally hearing Jesus like the disciples did. They probably sat around the campfire in a circle. In these relaxed times alone, Jesus shared truth they could apply in their lives. They would ask him questions He would gladly answer. When I read the Bible, I feel that same warmth, peace, insight, and friendship as Jesus speaks to me.

Soap: It says in Psalm 119:11, "I have hidden your word in my heart that I might not sin against you." Studying God's word keeps me from sinning. I once went to a retreat and the speaker said the Bible is like handing a bar of soap to the Holy Spirit to keep you clean. What if you didn't take a bath or shower? You would stink, people wouldn't come near you, and your health would deteriorate. The same happens to our spiritual life. It would stink, and we wouldn't attach anyone to God and our relationship to Him would deteriorate.

Diamond: Even though, I've read the same verse many times, I haven't gotten bored. That's because the Bible is like a diamond. Depending on where you stand relative to it, from its various facets, it displays different light and colors. Try looking at a well-cut diamond sometime. It's hard to describe and fascinating to see. The Bible is the same. Verses take on different meaning and come alive in different ways depending on where you are in life and how the Holy Spirit is leading you in understanding. About fifteen years ago, God brought to my attention Ephesians 4:29, "Do not let any unwholesome talk come out of your mouths, but only what is helpful for building others up according to their needs, that it may benefit those who listen." Even though, I had read it many times before, it took on a deeper meaning specific to me and inspired me in a different ministry direction. Without it, I wouldn't be writing this book. As you read the Bible, I'm certain diamonds will jump out at you as well.

Flashlight: In camping at night, it is very important to have a flashlight. It keeps you from getting lost. It says in Psalm 119:105, "Your word is a lamp for my feet, a light on my path." We live in a dark world. God's word is our flashlight to help us from getting lost.

Owner's Manual: As an engineer, it is easy for me to understand the concept of God is the Creator and we are the creation. Engineers create products to be useful for people. Working for a car company, we try to make things work well for customers and provide an owner's manual to help them know how to use and maintain the car as designed. My guess is probably the percentage of people who read their owner's manual are similar as the percentage that read their Bible. Sometimes, this leads to improper use or maintenance. In these cases, the customer finds out too late to avoid big problems. Another aspect is sometimes there are features that are available, but since the customer is unaware of them, they miss out on the benefits. How many times have we said after using a product for some time, "Wow, I never knew it could do that?" or "I wish I had known that earlier!" Also, when something needs assembled, we think we can put it together without instructions. This often leads to frustration and wasted time. It says in 2 Timothy 3:16, "All Scripture is God-breathed and is useful for teaching, rebuking, correcting and training in righteousness." The Bible is our instruction manual God the creator provides us to show how to properly live out our lives as He intended.

Romance Novel: Romance novels are the largest segment of fiction books at about 13 percent of sales, 90 percent are read by women. Two main reasons are as an antidote to stress and for mental escape. The Bible is a romance novel. It starts with God creating the ideal world and having a perfect relationship with Adam and Eve. Then Adam and Eve sinned and God's perfect creation and our relationship to Him fell apart. The rest of the Bible is where God reached out in love to solve the problem of sin. Through the blood of Jesus, He became ours for us to pay the price of sin. Then in the book of Revelation, God shows He's going to recreate the perfect world again and reign here on earth with all of his followers. Rather that escaping, the Bible shows what life is all about and how God loves us. What a relief for stress!

Shape Knife: I carve occasionally. One key to good carving is a sharp knife. Most knives are sharp but not enough for carving. If you ever tried carving with an ordinary pocket knife, you know what I mean. Carving knives are razor sharp. You have to be careful not to cut yourself and even wear gloves for protection. It says in Hebrews 4:12, "For the word of God is alive and active. Sharper than any double-edged sword, it penetrates even to dividing soul and spirit, joints and marrow; it judges the thoughts and attitudes of the heart." In Revelation 1:16, the double-edged sword is described as coming out of the mouth of Jesus. It says in Ephesians 6:17, "Take the helmet of salvation and the sword of the Spirit, which is the word of God." It says in Isaiah 55:11, "So is my word that goes out from my mouth: It will not return to me empty, but will accomplish what I desire and achieve the purpose for which I sent it." Because scripture comes from Jesus, Almighty God, His words have real power. For a year, a supervisor I know was not approaching someone in the group about a performance issue. He was frustrated, but wasn't comfortable approaching the person. Many times, I gave him advice and urged him to take action. He never did. I finally wrote down two verses related to the situation and gave them to him on a sticky note. I asked him to look them up and consider God's viewpoint. I'm not even sure about his relationship to God, but he looked them up, read them, and to my surprise, took action! I was humbly reminded of the power of God's double-edged sword.

Rudder: Even though rudders are small compared to the rest of the ship, they are needed to steer them in the right direction. Imagine you're on a ship in the middle of the ocean on a clear calm day. You can't see land in any direction. Also, your rudder is broken and you don't know it. You're essentially drifting. All seems well, so you're not worried. You don't realize you're way off course, headed for a storm and the rocks. In 2 Kings 22 and 23 is someone like this. In the interest of time, I'll paraphrase. It's about King Josiah who was one of the good kings of Judah. He tried to do right in God's eyes. Josiah requested the priest of the Temple of God to hire men to repair it. While working, the priest found the Book of the Law. He gave it to King Josiah's official who read it to the king. The king was shocked because the book said disaster was coming because he and his ancestors worshipped other gods and tolerated idol worship in the land. So upset, he tore his robes and cried. He ordered his officials to immediately inquire of God. They found a prophet who said God was going to bring disaster to the nation because of their idol worship. However, since King Josiah showed remorse and humbled himself, God would spare him and the people. The king immediately took action. He read the Book of the Law to all the people and led them to commit to following it and tore down all the places idol worship occurred. He was praised by God for this. Although King Josiah was good and followed God, he didn't realize his kingdom was polluted with idolatry. He was content caring for his own church yet tolerating idol worship. Not until he found the Book of the Law did he realize he did not measure up to God's standard. Once he knew God's Word, it motivated him to change quickly. Without the revelation of God's Word, Josiah and his nation would have innocently, contently drifted to disaster. The Bible reveals the right course for our lives and helps steer us toward it. Let's not be content playing church but really be those who seek to glorify God.

Elephant Sandwich: How do you eat an elephant? One bite at a time. There was a man who visited his friend's cabin. They went on a hike. When they reached a ravine, he pointed out a house on the other side. The house was surrounded by beautiful flowers. Amazed, the man asked his friend how it was accomplished. Did the government or a company come one day and plant all the flowers? He said there was an old couple who have lived there for many years. Year after year, they would plant some flowers. After many years of doing this a little bit persistently, you now enjoy the final result. This illustrates accomplishing great things requires doing little things consistently. The Bible is a large book. It has 66 books, 1,189 chapters, 31,173 verses, and 773,692 words. There are many benefits to regular reading of the Bible as I've pointed out, but faced with the enormous task may scare many away. Even though the Bible is the best-selling book of all time. So far 500 billion have been sold worldwide and 5 billion printed each year. The real question is how many have been read? I suspect many are collecting dust on coffee tables and bookshelves. Regular small bites keep this from happening to your Bible. To read the Bible in a year means 2,012 words per day. My experience is it would take fifteen minutes a day or the same amount time as commercials on a one-hour TV show. Why not DVR the show, then read the Bible for fifteen minutes, then watch the show by fast-forwarding through the commercials. Not such a big deal. My own experience is I had two hurdles. First, the translation was hard to understand. I found a translation I liked. My next hurdle was not being an avid reader (Why is this guy writing a book?). I purchased dramatized Bible CDs (these days, there are apps). They were word for word with different voices and sound effects. Since my daily commute was a half hour one way on a light traffic highway, I found I had a perfect personal space to be alone with God to listen and talk to Him. I would listen to the Bible for twenty minutes and pray the last ten minutes. This worked for me. The key is to find what works for you and do it consistently. Sometimes, we get frustrated because we don't hear God. My experience is this occurs when we stop reading His Word. It's like we're screaming to God to speak with us while we have our hands firmly over our ears. By reading God's word, we hear Him. Finally, just like any friend, we have to communicate to grow the relationship. I hope you're already consistently reading the Bible and enjoying the benefits. However, statistics show likely many of you are in the majority. Do you want God to be intimate with you, to regularly cleanse you, to reveal to you, to keep you from getting lost, to teach you how to live, to remind you he loves you, to give you His power and to keep your life on course? If you answered yes, start taking regular small bites of God's Word!

Next Step: Reflection, Application, and Action

Not at all ⓪ — Slightly ② — Some ④ — Much ⑥ — Very Much ⑧ — Perfect =Jesus ⑩

Ask God to reveal where you are, what to do next, and to help you (five or below should take action).

Priority	Basic Question	Statement	Rating	Action to Improve	New Rating	Difference in Rating
God First		I study the Bible regularly.				

CHAPTER 6

The 5Ws and H of Prayer

This chapter is titled "The 5 Ws and H of Prayer." Earlier, we learned God has provided the Bible, prayer, Holy Spirit, and the church. This chapter, I want to focus on prayer.

Why: First I want to talk about why prayer is important. To find out why prayer is important, let's look at some scripture. It says in Psalm 141:2, "May my prayer be set before you like incense; may the lifting up of my hands be like the evening sacrifice." Revelation 5:8 says, "And when he had taken the scroll, the four living creatures and the twenty-four elders fell down before the Lamb. Each one had a harp and they were holding golden bowls full of incense, which are the prayers of God's people." Proverbs 15:8 says, "The Lord detests the sacrifice of the wicked, but the prayers of the upright pleases him." The reason we should pray is because it pleases God. They are so precious He stores them in golden bowls and they are a sweet perfume before Him. Do you want to please God? Then pray. God loves hearing from His beloved children.

Who: Who should pray? Paul said in 1 Timothy 2:7–8, "And for this purpose I was appointed a herald and an apostle—I am telling the truth, I am not lying—and a true and faithful teacher of the Gentiles. Therefore I want men everywhere to pray, lifting up holy hands without anger or disputing." God wants everyone to pray!

When: Let's discuss when should we pray. Describing the early Christians, it says in Acts 2:42, "They devoted themselves to prayer." It says in Romans 12:12, "Be faithful in prayer." It says in 1 Thessalonians 5:17–18, "Pray continuously, give thanks in all circumstances; for this is God's will for you in Christ Jesus." It says in Colossians 4:2, "Devote yourselves to prayer, being watchful and thankful." It's clear we should pray regularly. We should ask ourselves is there any day of the year we don't need to please God or don't need to talk with Him? I think when we answer this question, it makes sense we should make time daily to pray.

Where: Now let's talk about where to pray The answer comes from the following verses. Matthew 6:5–6 says, "And when you pray, do not be like the hypocrites, for they love to pray standing in the synagogues and on the street corners to be seen by others. Truly I tell you they have received their reward in full. But when you pray go into your room, close the door and pray to your Father, who is unseen. Then your Father, who sees what is done in secret, will reward you." Matthew 14:23 says, "After he had dismissed them, he went up on a mountainside by himself to pray. Later that night he was there alone." Mark 1:35 says, "Very early in the morning while it was still dark, Jesus got up, left the house and went to a solitary place, where he prayed." Mark 6:46 says, "After leaving them, he went upon a mountainside to pray." Luke 5:16 says, "But Jesus often withdrew to lonely places and prayed." Luke 6:12 says, "One of those days Jesus went out to a mountainside to pray, and spent the night praying to God." It's clear we should find a quiet place to pray. God wants intimate conversation with us and having a quiet place alone provides this. This is not saying we shouldn't pray as a group or public setting, but our regular daily prayers are enhanced when we are alone with God. When we are alone with God, we can focus more easily. As an example, I pray in my car on the way to work. I drive a long stretch of highway without much traffic. I'm alone in my car with God. Find what works for you!

How: Let's get into how we should pray. First, I want to talk about the speaking style. It says in Matthew 6:7–8, "And when you pray, do not keep on babbling like pagans, for they think they will be heard because of their many words. Do not be like them, for your Father knows what you need before you ask him." Then in Luke 20:45 & 47, "While all the people were listening, Jesus said to his disciples, 'Beware of the teachers of the law for a show make lengthy prayers. These men will be punished most severely.'" These verses remind us to pray to God in a conversational style like we would to any friend. Once I went to Japan for two weeks. There was one particular guy who I worked with who spoke very little English and I spoke even less Japanese, so we had a difficult time communicating. I was amazed at the karaoke bar, he sang only English songs and knew all the words and pronounced them perfectly. I still wonder how he did it and would love to talk with him about it, but we fundamentally don't speak the same language. We can sometimes pray in a karaoke style. It sounds and looks good, but it's not genuine and, in the end, isn't effective communication with God. When I'm alone in my car, I pray out loud where no one but God hears me. This helps me to focus and helps me to have genuine conversation with God. I imagine God is sitting next to me so my prayers are more conversational. We've had many great discussions. You need to have genuine discussions with God. The next topic is our attitude as we pray. In Luke 18:1–8, "Then Jesus told his disciples a parable to show them they should always pray and not give up. He said: 'In a certain town there was a judge who neither feared God nor cared what people thought. And there was a widow in that town who kept coming to him with the plea, 'Grant me justice against my adversary.' For some time he refused. But finally he said to himself, 'Even though I don't fear God or care what people think, yet because this widow keeps bothering me, I will see that she gets justice, so that she won't eventually come and attack me!' And the Lord said, 'Listen to what the unjust judge says. And will not God bring about justice for his chosen ones, who cry out to him day and night? Will he keep putting them off? I tell you, he will see that they get justice, and quickly. However, when the Son of Man comes, will he find faith on the earth?'" Then in Luke 11:5–13, "Then Jesus said to them, 'Suppose you have a friend, and you go to him at midnight and say, "Friend, lend me three loaves of bread; a friend of mine on a journey has come to me, and I have no food to offer him." And suppose the one inside answers, "Don't bother me. The door is already locked, and my children and I are in bed. I can't get up and give you anything." I tell you, even though he will not get up and give you the bread because of friendship, yet because of your shameless audacity[a] he will surely get up and give you as much as you need." In Luke 11:9–13, "So I say to you: Ask and it will be given to you; seek and you will find; knock and the door will be opened to you. For everyone who asks receives; the one who seeks finds; and to the one who knocks, the door will be opened. Which of you fathers, if your son asks for[b] a fish, will give him a snake instead? Or if he asks for an egg, will give him a scorpion? If you then, though you are evil, know how to give good gifts to your children, how much more will your Father in heaven give the Holy Spirit to those who ask him!" Matthew 21:21–22 says, "Jesus replied, 'Truly I tell you, if you have faith and do not doubt, not only can you do what was done to the fig tree, but also you can say to this mountain, 'Go, throw yourself into the sea,' and it will be done. If you believe, you will receive whatever you ask for in prayer." In Mark 11:22–24, it says, "'Have faith in God,' Jesus answered. 'Truly[a] I tell you, if anyone says to this mountain, "Go, throw yourself into the sea," and does not doubt in their heart but believes that what they say will happen, it will be done for them. Therefore I tell you, whatever you ask for in prayer, believe that you have received it, and it will be yours.'" In James 1:5–8, it says, "If any of you lacks wisdom, you should ask God, who gives generously to all without finding fault, and it will be given to you. But when you ask, you must believe and not doubt, because the one who doubts is like a wave of the sea, blown and tossed by the wind. That person should not expect to receive anything from the Lord. Such a person is double-minded and unstable in all they do." All of these verses point to three attitudes we should have when we pray. We should be bold and believe what we ask will be answered by God, be humble and be persistent.

How and What: Now let's discuss the how and what we should pray about. Let's read the following verses and break them down. Jesus said in Matthew 6:9–15, "This, then, is how you should pray: 'Our Father in heaven, hallowed be your name, your kingdom come, your will be done, on earth as it is in heaven. Give us today our daily bread. And forgive us our debts, as we also have forgiven our debtors. And lead us not into temptation,[a] but deliver us from the evil one.[b]' For if you forgive other people when they sin against you, your heavenly Father will also forgive you. But if you do not forgive others their sins, your Father will not forgive your sins."

Let's break this down:

Our Father: It reminds us that we are not alone and are part of a family. God is significant to us and is our protector and provider. It puts our relationship in proper perspective. He is the Father and we are the children.

In heaven: It reminds us God is above us, that heaven exists as well as hell.

Hallowed be your name: It reminds us God is special, holy, and we should honor Him.

In this section, Jesus is teaching us to seek God's face and to praise Him for who He is and how special He is to us. We should thank Him for answered prayer or special blessings He's given us. In the Bible, it says, "Pride comes before the fall." When things are going well, we tend to forget about God and discount the role He's played in our success and that starts the beginning of our downfall. This happened to the Israelites over and over: things went well, they forgot about God, God brought an enemy against them, they cried out to God, and God sent a judge to rescue them. After everything was well again, the cycle would start all over again. This is true of the nation of Israel and true of us as individuals as well. When we pray daily, praising and thanking God, we can prevent this cycle.

Your kingdom come, your will be done, on earth as it is in heaven: Reminds us to cry out to God to make it happen. When we do this, we align ourselves with God's ultimate plan for Jesus to return to abolish sin, recreate the world like it was before sin, and to bring His kingdom down to earth to be with all His believers. Also, it should make us think about and ask God to help us do what we can do to help fulfill Jesus's command to go tell others about him and disciple them. This is a perfect opportunity to talk to God about your own ministry to family, community, and world. President Kennedy said, "Ask not what your country can do for you, but ask what you can do for your country." Before we ask for our needs from God, we should ask what can we do to build God's kingdom.

In conclusion in this section, we see God's face as we praise, thank, and look for ways to build His kingdom.

Give us this day our daily bread: This reminds us to ask God for our needs. These needs can cover the whole spectrum of requests. They include mental, physical, and spiritual needs for us and others. Just like the Israelites had manna each day and couldn't gather more than a day's portion or it would spoil. We need to focus on what we need today. Honestly, most of us don't need a reminder. We tend to pray only when we have needs and only pray about needs.

And forgive our debts as we forgive our debtors. And lead us not into temptation, but deliver us from the evil one: This reminds us we are accountable for our sins, to bring them to God, to forgive others, to ask for God's help to prevent further sin. This area we tend to shy away from because in our human nature these things are hard to approach God about. Let's look at some scripture to understand why this is important. Second Chronicles 7:14 says, "If my people, who are called by my name, will humble themselves and pray and seek my face and turn from their wicked ways, then I will hear from heaven, and I will forgive their sin and will heal their land." Proverbs 28:9 says, "If anyone turns a deaf ear to my instruction, even their prayers are detestable." Isaiah 1:15 says, "When you spread out your hands in prayer, I hide my eyes from you; even when you offer many prayers, I am not listening." Mark 11:25 says "And when you stand praying, if you hold anything against anyone, forgive them, so that your Father in heaven may forgive you your sins." These verses show that when we fail to repent of our sins and forgive others for their sins against us, it hinders our prayers. In other words, God won't hear them. Another related verse is Luke 6:28, "Bless those who curse you, pray for those who mistreat you." It's tough to deal with some people such as coworkers, etc., who make us miserable. I've had situations like this and someone suggested I pray for the individual. I didn't pray they would stop making me miserable, but for their needs. I found although it's hard to do, it gradually changed my attitude and helped me see them the way God sees them. The bottom line is if we do not ask forgiveness, seek God's help to change us, and not forgive others, we inhibit our growth to become more like Christ and our prayers never go above the ceiling.

In conclusion, this section, we are seeking God's hand in providing our needs, forgiving, and helping us overcome sin.

For yours is the Kingdom, the Power, and the Glory. Amen: This part is actually not in the Bible. Bible scholars added it because in most prayers, the end usually concludes with praising God. This reminds us that it's all about God and it's our chance to praise Him again. We again seek His face. So the example prayer Jesus taught us teaches us to

1. Praise and thank God.
2. Talk to Him about how we can help bring about His kingdom down on earth.
3. Ask Him to supply our/others' needs.
4. Repent and seek help to prevent sin in your life.
5. Forgive others.
6. Praise Him again.

We seek His face, then His hands, and then His face. Kind of like an Oreo cookie. You may remember the Tootsie Pop commercials where they ask the wise old owl professor how many licks does it take to get to the caramel of the center of the Tootsie Pop. After three licks, he can't resist and crunches through the candy shell to the center. Then he proclaims "Three!" We often pray like that. We always want to pray for our needs, but want to rush or forget about the rest. We love to seek God's hands, but may neglect his face. Think about it this way. If you had a friend and the only time they contacted you was only when they needed something or only interested in what you can do for them, you probably wouldn't have a very strong friendship. When we do this, we think of God as a heavenly bellhop or a genie in a bottle. When we do this, our prayers often don't get higher than the ceiling.

The last point I want to make involves Daniel 6. In the interest of time, I will paraphrase. Daniel had distinguished himself as a leader in the Persian empire. The king planned to put him in charge of all the other leaders. Some of the leaders were jealous and looked for dirt on Daniel to discredit him. They couldn't find anything wrong because Daniel had integrity. They decided the only way to ruin Daniel was through his relationship with God. They approached the king and had him pass a law that for the next thirty days, no one could pray to anyone except the king. Once enacted, the law could not be repealed. The penalty for breaking the law was to be thrown into the lions' den. When Daniel heard about it, he went home and, as usual, opened his windows pointing toward Jerusalem and prayed to God three times a day. The other leaders caught him praying and brought him to the king. Although the king liked Daniel, he could not violate his own law, so he ordered him thrown into the lions' den in the evening and put a stone over the top. Before Daniel was put in, the king said, "May your God, whom you serve continually rescue you!"

The king could hardly sleep for worry. At the first light of dawn, the king got up and hurried to the lions' den. When he came near the den, he called to Daniel in an anguished voice, "Daniel, servant of the living God, has your God, whom you serve continually, been able to rescue you from the lions?"

Daniel answered, "May the king live forever! My God sent his angels and he shut the mouths of the lions. They have not hurt me because I was found innocent in his sight. Nor have I ever done wrong before you, Your Majesty."

The king was overjoyed. He ordered the men who plotted against Daniel and their families thrown into the lions' den. The lions were hungry. Then the king wrote a decree that all people must fear and reverence the God of Daniel. Would you like to be like Daniel and please God by praying daily, alone, having intimate conversation, approaching God with faith, boldness, humility, and persistence, seeking both His face as well as His hands! I hope you will pray just like Daniel to strenghten your relationship with God, become more like Christ and, positively affect our families and communities.

Next Step: Reflection, Application, and Action

Not at all (0) — Slightly (2) — Some (4) — Much (6) — Very Much (8) — Perfect =Jesus (10)

Ask God to reveal where you are, what to do next, and to help you (five or below should take action).

Priority	Basic Question	Statement	Rating	Action to Improve	New Rating	Difference in Rating
First: God	Am I strengthening my relationship with God?	I pray regularly.				

CHAPTER 7

No Respect

Previously, I spoke to you how God wants us to have the character of Christ, and he uses four things synchronized together to help us develop. These are the Bible, prayer, Holy Spirit, and church. We've already talked about the Bible and prayer. This chapter's message is "No Respect." My favorite comedian is Rodney Dangerfield. His famous line was "I don't get no respect." Most of his jokes were about not getting any respect from his parents, family, and others. In many people's minds, the Holy Spirit can be perceived this way. We can easily see the Father's great works like creating the world and bringing down plagues on Egypt. We see the miracles Jesus performed and His resurrection. It's easy to recognize their activities, but the activity of the Holy Spirit is not as apparent. Maybe because He doesn't have his words highlighted in red in the Bible or He's listed last in order…Father, Son, Holy Spirit. If we have any understanding, I think we can at least remember Jesus talking about sending the Holy Spirt after He went up to heaven. It seems He comes late in the story after most of God's plan has played out. However, what I discovered He is mentioned 317 times in the Bible, 72 times in the Old Testament. He is first mentioned in Genesis 1:2, "Now the earth was formless and empty, darkness was over the surface of the deep, and the Spirit of God was hovering over the waters." We see that the

Holy Spirit was there from the beginning of the creation of the earth. Next let's discuss why the Holy Spirit is important to us. Looking at Genesis 1:26, "Then God said, 'Let us make mankind in our image, in our likeness, so that they may rule over the fish in the sea and the birds in the sky, over the livestock and all the wild animals,[a] and over all the creatures that move along the ground.'" In the creation story, we see the word us. This verse tells us we are not made like the other creation and have special characteristics that are like God. That doesn't mean we are the same as God, but have similar characteristics. Just like any child who gets characteristics from each parent. Perhaps looks, abilities, and personality. From the Father, we inherit free will and dominion over creation. From the Son, a physical body. We can identify with Jesus because he relates to us in a physical world. We can understand with our physical senses. In other words, he walked in our shoes. He could die like we will and he can rise again with a body that never dies. His resurrected body is not like ours. He came out of tightly wrapped burial clothes without breaking them. He was able to suddenly appear to those walking to Emmaus and then disappear. He was able to walk through walls to appear to His disciples and He was able to ascend to heaven on a cloud. That's the body we will have someday if we believe in Jesus as our Lord and Savior. It doesn't say what our new body will be, but we do know that it will be different than the one we have now. I'm looking forward to this! From the Holy Spirit, we receive a spirit or soul. This is the real us that never dies. How do we know we have a spiritual component? It says in Genesis 2:7, "Then the Lord God formed a man[a] from the dust of the ground and breathed into his nostrils the breath of life, and the man became a living being." We can see God breathed His Spirit into man and we became alive. Up to that point, he was just a pile of dirt. Also, as I mentioned earlier, there are 317 verses in the Bible about the Holy Spirit. There are also 249 verses that talk about the small *s* spirit. In my own experiences, I've seen loved ones pass away. The amazing thing is at the very moment of passing, they look like an empty shell. Let's look at Luke 23:42–43, "Then he said, 'Jesus, remember me when you come into your kingdom.[a]' Jesus answered him, 'Truly I tell you, today you will be with me in paradise.'" Obviously Jesus was talking about the thief's living spirit and not his dead body. Our physical body here on earth carries our spirit, the real us, which lives forever, just like a pop can carries pop. Also, it says in Ephesians 6:12, "For our struggle is not against flesh and blood, but against the rulers, against the authorities, against the powers of this dark world and against the spiritual forces of evil in the heavenly realms." Since we really deal in the spiritual realm, it makes sense that to truly understand God requires Spirit to spirit communication. We can't see Him physically, but He is there. Just like the wind, we can't see it, but can see its effects. It's important to realize the Holy Spirit's existence and His role in drawing us to God. One analogy is an engine. We all recognize the engine block, piston, etc. Often, we forget about the oil. It keeps all the parts working together smoothly. Try to run an engine without oil and see what happens. It will heat up and seize. The Holy Spirit is the oil in our lives which helps us understand God and to do our part in building His kingdom. He's the power source that makes things happen. When God said let there be light, He made it happen. He was the one who came over Mary and she conceived Jesus. Now let's talk about His role more specifically.

When Jesus was about to ascend into heaven, His disciples undoubtedly didn't want Him to leave. He said to them in John 16:7–11, "But very truly I tell you, it is for your good that I am going away. Unless I go away, the Advocate will not come to you; but if I go, I will send him to you. When he comes, he will prove the world to be in the wrong about sin and righteousness and judgment: about sin, because people do not believe in me; about righteousness, because I am going to the Father, where you can see me no longer; and about judgment, because the prince of this world now stands condemned."

We see His role is to communicate the need for salvation and invite us to accept Jesus as Lord and Savior. Even though someone told you the gospel the Holy Spirit communicated to your spirit this truth and appealed to you to accept it. Jesus said to Nicodemus, a Pharisee, in John 3:3–6, "Jesus replied, 'Very truly I tell you, no one can see the kingdom of God unless they are born again.[a]' 'How can someone be born when they are old?' Nicodemus asked. 'Surely they cannot enter a second time into their mother's womb to be born!' Jesus answered, 'Very truly I tell you, no one can enter the kingdom of God unless they are born of water and the Spirit. Flesh gives birth to flesh, but the Spirit[b] gives birth to spirit." It is through the rebirth of our spirit we are reunited with God. Jesus said in Matthew 12:31–32, "And so I tell you, every kind of sin and slander can be forgiven, but blasphemy against the Spirit will not be forgiven. Anyone who speaks a word against the Son of Man will be forgiven, but anyone who speaks against the Holy Spirit will not be forgiven, either in this age or in the age to come." These verses show that we can sin against Jesus and will be forgiven. In fact, some even murdered Him, yet He would forgive them if they asked for forgiveness and accepted Him as Lord and Savior. Paul is a great example of this. He was a Pharisee and was actively hunting Christians down. While on one of these trips, he met Jesus on the road to Damascus. He realized the truth and became a Christian. Led by God, he became the first missionary to the nations beyond Israel and wrote thirteen of the twenty-seven books of the New Testament. In the Old Testament, we see similar examples. Before the Ten Commandments were brought down by Moses, the Israelites were already breaking all of them. Once they were in the land they constantly drifted from God, He would bring another nation against them, they would cry out and He would help them. What could we possibly do to the Holy Spirit which we could never be forgiven? It goes back to His role. I took a class once about evangelism. One of the things they said was on average, a person will hear the Gospel on average seven times before they accept it. Now if we reject the Holy Spirit's message the first time, will he never forgive us? Of course not! The role of the Holy Spirit is to bring truth to each of us. If we reject Him our entire lives and die without accepting it, then this cannot be forgiven. Talk about ultimate respect! In my own case, when I was accepting the Gospel, I remember a feeling like something was tugging at my heart. I've heard others describe it that way as well. What I thought was heartburn or indigestion was really the Holy Spirit convincing me of the truth. Now let's talk about the next role. Once we have accepted Jesus, then the role of the Holy

Spirit is to transform us. It says in 1 Peter 1:16, "For it is written: 'Be holy, because I am holy.'" The character of the Holy Spirit is described in Galatians 5:22–23, "But the fruit of the Spirit is love, joy, peace, forbearance, kindness, goodness, faithfulness, gentleness and self-control." The Holy Spirit is called Holy because He himself has these attributes. However, it doesn't stop there. He wants us to have them too and is willing to help us achieve them. That would be like Jack Nicklaus saying to you or me, "I have the skills that make me the greatest golfer of all time, and I'm willing to teach them to you one on one so that you can acquire them too." Wow, God as our personal trainer! Let's break this down a little further. Let's look at John 16:12–13, "I have much more to say to you, more than you can now bear. But when he, the Spirit of truth, comes, he will guide you into all the truth. He will not speak on his own; he will speak only what he hears, and he will tell you what is yet to come." It's clear the role of the Holy Spirit is to bring God's truth to us, to give us wisdom, and to help us understand it. Where I worked, there were both Americans and Japanese. We often had meetings together. Interpreters helped us understand each other. Even though they seemed invisible to us, we couldn't work effectively without them. The Holy Spirit is our interpreter to help us understand the wisdom of God and us to apply it specifically to our lives. The Bible is an amazing book. What amazes me is I've never heard of a book you can read over and over again and get new meaning from it each time. Seems like magic! As I mentioned previously, I don't like reading the same book twice, but not so with the Bible. What makes it different and special is the authors were inspired by God. Jesus is called the Word so we are reading the words of Jesus Himself. The other thing that makes it special is you can read the same passage several times, but then it will jump off the page and hit you between the eyes at exactly the right time in your life. It seems like luck, coincidence, or magic, but it's really the Holy Spirit helping us to understand. Additionally, He helps us have discernment so we can experience what it says in Philippians 4:7, "And the peace of God, which transcends all understanding, will guard your hearts and your minds in Christ Jesus." What this means in a crisis as we look around from our human perspective, we become afraid and panic. However, through spiritual eyes, we are calm. Has this ever happened to you? It has to me. The best example in the Bible is when the Prophet Elisha is surrounded by an enemy army. Hi assistant panics. Elisha tells him there are more protecting them than the enemy army. The assistant still panics. Elisha asks God to open the assistant's eyes. The assistant sees what Elisha sees that they are surrounded by countless angels. I'm sure Elisha had peace that surpasses understanding that day and his assistant eventually did too. Remember, peace is one of the fruits of the Spirit. Also it says in Psalm 23, "Even though I walk through the darkest valley, [a]I will fear no evil, for you are with me; your rod and your staff, they comfort me." We often use this verse when someone is about to die or spoken at a funeral, but it's very true every day. Now let's look at the last role of the Holy Spirit. It says in 1 Corinthians 12:4–7, 11, "There are different kinds of gifts, but the same Spirit distributes them. There are different kinds of service, but the same Lord. There are different kinds of working, but in all of them and in everyone it is the same God at work. Now to each one the manifestation of the Spirit is given for the common good." All these are the work of one and the same Spirit, and he distributes them to each one, just as he determines. We see he provides us with Spiritual gifts which are supernatural abilities and skills to carry out the work to build God's kingdom. Jesus said just before He ascended into heaven in Acts 1:8, "But you will receive power when the Holy Spirit comes on you; and you will be my witnesses in Jerusalem, and in all Judea and Samaria, and to the ends of the earth." This is a God-sized mission for us and only through God's enabled abilities do we have any hope to accomplish it. These gifts are given at the moment we accept Jesus as Lord and Savior. All believers have at least one and maybe others as the Holy Spirit deems necessary. To God, we are not just numbers and are not treated in an assembly line fashion. God knows us as individuals and he carefully selects gifts specifically tailored to us to fulfill our role. When I was a new Christian and first heard about this was when a class was offered on knowing your spiritual gifts. It sounded weird like some kind of voodoo. I took the class and found out it wasn't the case. I think many Christians are armed and dangerous, but aren't aware of it. We need to first understand which gifts we have and then learn how to use them. The Holy Spirit helps us with this. Two verses of caution: Ephesians 4:30, "And do not grieve the Holy Spirit of God, with whom you were sealed for the day of redemption." Also 1 Thessalonians 5:19, "Do not quench the Spirit." These verses remind us that because of our free will, we can choose to cooperate with the Holy Spirit or not. In our analogy of Jack Nicklaus, he is there and offers to personally teach us. If we say no, he won't force himself on us. The Holy Spirit is the same way. Do you want to be saved, become more like Jesus, and have supernatural abilities to build God's kingdom, then open up your self to the Holy Spirit. I once was on a trip and stopped for gas. I noticed the usual choices of octane, but next to these was 110 octane. I though wow I might have to try this. I looked a little closer and it said, "Racing fuel: don't use in ordinary cars." I didn't try it, but I wondered how much extra power I would get. I imagined screaming down the highway like a dragster! Our lives are like this. If we haven't accepted Jesus as our Lord and Savior, we don't even have any fuel, so we're going nowhere fast. Even if we are, we may just be sputtering around in life. Do you want your Christian life to be supercharged by filling your spiritual gas tank with the Holy Spirit? By inviting Him to guide and counsel you into all truth and provide you abilities to do the exciting work of God, this will happen. Do this by

1. Accepting Jesus as Lord and Savior and be born of the Spirit;
2. Reading your Bible daily and anticipate and apply verses that jump out at you;
3. Praying daily and anticipate the Holy Spirit to help you discern the answer;
4. Plugging into a body of believers such as church, Sunday school, Bible study, etc., and let the Holy Spirt lead you to truth;
5. Discovering and use your spiritual gifts. There are several free websites which provide questionnaires which you can

take. Also, trying different ministries in your church and elsewhere.

I hope all of you are doing these things already and that your Christian life is growing and has the vitality the Holy Spirit wants you to have. If not, it's time to understand and respect His role in our lives and make the changes to get moving.

CHAPTER 8

From Hundredth to First

Previously, we talked about the Four Horsemen and that they help you to grow in relationship to God and become more like Jesus. They are the Bible, prayer, Holy Spirit, and church. Since we covered the first three, we will wrap up with church. This chapter is titled "From Hundredth to First." In golf, there are one hundred individual golfers that vie to be first place. Sometimes, we view church the same way. We see all the church buildings with different names on them in the same neighborhoods, yet we don't see them as one church, but different. This makes the individual churches not cooperate and share resources. Taking a 10,000-foot view, we see there is one leader and head of the church. That would be Jesus and one church. In the New Testament, the church began the day of Pentecost, a Jewish religious holiday and coincidently fifty days after the resurrection of Jesus. Jews scattered all over the world would come to Jerusalem to worship. Let's see how the Bible describes that day. In Acts 2:1–15, 21–24, 36–41, "When the day of Pentecost came, they were all together in one place. Suddenly a sound like the blowing of a violent wind came from heaven and filled the whole house where they were sitting. They saw what seemed to be tongues of fire that separated and came to rest on each of them. All of them were filled with the Holy Spirit and began to speak in other tongues[a] as the Spirit enabled them. Now there were staying in Jerusalem God fearing Jews from every nation under heaven. When they heard this sound, a crowd came together in bewilderment, because each one heard their own language being spoken. Utterly amazed, they asked: 'Aren't all these who are speaking Galileans? Then how is it that each of us hears them in our native language? Parthians, Medes and Elamites; residents of Mesopotamia, Judea and Cappadocia, Pontus and Asia,[b] Phrygia and Pamphylia, Egypt and the parts of Libya near Cyrene; visitors from Rome (both Jews and converts to Judaism); Cretans and Arabs—we hear them declaring the wonders of God in our own tongues!' Amazed and perplexed, they asked one another, 'What does this mean?' Some, however, made fun of them and said, 'They have had too much wine.' Then Peter stood up with the Eleven, raised his voice and addressed the crowd: 'Fellow Jews and all of you who live in Jerusalem, let me explain this to you; listen carefully to what I say. These people are not drunk, as you suppose. It's only nine in the morning! And everyone who calls on the name of the Lord will be saved.'[c] 'Fellow Israelites, listen to this: Jesus of Nazareth was a man accredited by God to you by miracles, wonders and signs, which God did among you through him, as you yourselves know. This man was handed over to you by God's deliberate plan and foreknowledge; and you, with the help of wicked men,[d] put him to death by nailing him to the cross. But God raised him from the dead, freeing him from the agony of death, because it was impossible for death to keep its hold on him. Therefore let all Israel be assured of this: God has made this Jesus, whom you crucified, both Lord and Messiah.' When the people heard this, they were cut to the heart and said to Peter and the other apostles, 'Brothers, what shall we do?' Peter replied, 'Repent and be baptized, every one of you, in the name of Jesus Christ for the forgiveness of your sins. And you will receive the gift of the Holy Spirit. The promise is for you and your children and for all who are far off—for all whom the Lord our God will call.' With many other words he warned them; and he pleaded with them, 'Save yourselves from this corrupt generation.' Those who accepted his message were baptized, and about three thousand were added to their number that day." The word *church* is mentioned in the Bible

207 times. There are 7 main messages. From this passage, we see the church has one leader, Jesus; one message, the gospel; and a collection of believers of that Gospel. What you notice is Peter was the spokesman, but the other disciples stood with him. You didn't see them each taking a turn and giving their own version of the Gospel. The listeners heard one message albeit in their own language, which was a miracle of the Holy Spirit. The listeners not only spoke different languages, but undoubtedly came from different cultures, etc. That first day, the Church of Jesus Christ experienced tremendous growth. Later in Acts, we see especially churches being started especially by Paul and likely the seeds of those churches came from the three thousand added on the day of Pentecost as people returned home from this experience. We also see in Acts, the apostles worked together with all the churches to keep consistent practices. Paul especially wrote several letters to the churches to clarify or teach. This provided consistent direction to all churches. An example is when some of the apostles felt all church members should be circumcised like the Jews. After much discussion, they gave direction this was not required. Also, the churches worked together. One example was when they made a collection of money from all the churches to provide for one that was in need. Contrasting today, there are many churches that pretty much have Jesus Christ as head and pretty much have a similar Gospel and pretty much have similar practices. They are all governed separately. As a result, these pretty much add up to a lot of gray areas which then causes lack of cooperation, communication, and collaboration among churches worldwide. This causes a variety of issues such as redundancy. I guess you can say the church of Jesus Christ from back in the day of the Apostles to now has splintered. What can we do about this? First we have to have the mindset that finally even though there are differences, we have to think we are one church. We are not part of a building, but a worldwide church. We should encourage our church leadership to cooperate, communicate and collaborate as well has make a relationship with our churches working in the same mission field. This would strengthen the effectiveness of all the churches in building God's kingdom. In Matthew 9:37, "Then he said to his disciples, 'The harvest is plentiful but the

workers are few." One of the reasons for this is redundancy. Even though most churches have a lot more in common than differences when they don't work together, they water down their efforts and thus creating the situation where they reduce the workers. Next let's talk about what churches do. To illuminate this, let's read Matthew 25:31–46, "When the Son of Man comes in his glory, and all the angels with him, he will sit on his glorious throne. All the nations will be gathered before him, and he will separate the people one from another as a shepherd separates the sheep from the goats. He will put the sheep on his right and the goats on his left. Then the King will say to those on his right, 'Come, you who are blessed by my Father; take your inheritance, the kingdom prepared for you since the creation of the world. For I was hungry and you gave me something to eat, I was thirsty and you gave me something to drink, I was a stranger and you invited me in, I needed clothes and you clothed me, I was sick and you looked after me, I was in prison and you came to visit me.' Then the righteous will answer him, 'Lord, when did we see you hungry and feed you, or thirsty and give you something to drink? When did we see you a stranger and invite you in, or needing clothes and clothe you? When did we see you sick or in prison and go to visit you?' The King will reply, 'Truly I tell you, whatever you did for one of the least of these brothers and sisters of mine, you did for me.' Then he will say to those on his left, 'Depart from me, you who are cursed, into the eternal fire prepared for the devil and his angels. For I was hungry and you gave me nothing to eat, I was thirsty and you gave me nothing to drink, I was a stranger and you did not invite me in, I needed clothes and you did not clothe me, I was sick and in prison and you did not look after me.' They also will answer, 'Lord, when did we see you hungry or thirsty or a stranger or needing clothes or sick or in prison, and did not help you?' He will reply, 'Truly I tell you, whatever you did not do for one of the least of these, you did not do for me.' Then they will go away to eternal punishment, but the righteous to eternal life." This passage of scripture indicates we should care for Jesus and the way to do that is to care for people. The next scripture clarifies even further. First Corinthians 13:1–3 says, "If I speak in the tongues[a] of men or of angels, but do not have love, I am only a resounding gong or a clanging cymbal. If I have the gift of prophecy and can fathom all mysteries and all knowledge, and if I have a faith that can move mountains, but do not have love, I am nothing. If I give all I possess to the poor and give over my body to hardship that I may boast,[b] but do not have love, I gain nothing." This verse clearly indicates we are to care for people out of a motive of love. If our motive is not love, our effort is fruitless. So we are to love and care for God by loving and caring for people. However, which people? Let's look at Luke 10:30–37, "A man was going down from Jerusalem to Jericho, when he was attacked by robbers. They stripped him of his clothes, beat him and went away, leaving him half dead. A priest happened to be going down the same road, and when he saw the man, he passed by on the other side. So too, a Levite, when he came to the place and saw him, passed by on the other side. But a Samaritan, as he traveled, came where the man was; and when he saw him, he took pity on him. He went to him and bandaged his wounds, pouring on oil and wine. Then he put the man on his own donkey, brought him to an inn and took care of him. The next day he took out two denarii[e] and gave them to the innkeeper. 'Look after him,' he said, 'and when I return, I will reimburse you for any extra expense you may have.' Which of these three do you think was a neighbor to the man who fell into the hands of robbers? The expert in the law replied, 'The one who had mercy on him.' Jesus told him, 'Go and do likewise.'" We see the contrast between a Jew and a Samaritan. The Samaritan helps the Jew. However, in those days, Jews and Samaritan didn't associate with each other, so this parable illustrates the Samaritan showing unusual kindness toward the Jew. For the sake of our discussion, let's replace the Samaritan for the follower of Christ and the Jew as not a follower of Christ. Jesus wants us to love and care for those who are not believers. We are the only Jesus they will ever see as we act on His behalf as His hands, feet, arms, and legs. These acts of care rooted in love can help persuade them to become a follower of Jesus as well. Who else can we care for? It says in John 13:34, "A new command I give you: Love one another. As I have loved you, so you must love one another." When asked what are the two greatest commandments, Jesus said,

"Love God and love your neighbor as yourself." The neighbor was illustrated by the parable which we just looked at. However, just before he was arrested, he gave a new command to love and care for fellow followers of Jesus. One can only guess why Jesus emphasized this. It seems so obvious we need instruction on loving people who don't believe in the same things we believe and even will argue with us about it. However, in His final moments with His disciples, before his arrest, he takes time to remind them to love and care about fellow followers. In my observation in attending many different churches, I've noticed that church members tend to be harsh toward their fellow church members more than non-church members. Why is this? Maybe some people feel they are expected to keep a higher standard so they feel justified to rebuke fellow church members consistently. However, the receiver of the ire often feels rejected and does not feel the reaction is motivated by loved. I'm not saying we should never point out areas in a person's life that needs improving. However, it should be carefully done in an encouraging way and motivated by love. Otherwise, you have division and strife in the church. In summary, followers of Jesus Christ motivated by love should care for Jesus by caring for those who are not followers, as well as followers of Jesus Christ. Let's talk more about the word "care." This is not limited to the actions in Matthew 25. In the end, the ultimate purpose is to glorify God and build His kingdom. So it can be anything toward that end that is physical, material, mental, and spiritual. Anything that shows the other person the love of God. It can be something you do under the umbrella of the church activities or outside of the church activities. This description gives a very wide envelope of activities. Thinking about the church body as a human body, most of our time is spent in four categories. The largest two are working and resting (sleeping) and the two smaller are eating (feeding) and exercising. With this balance, you have a healthy human body and church body. Let's talk about each one and look at examples. Feeding, resting, and exercising are all aimed at strengthening the body. Things like reading your Bible, praying, church services attendance, Sunday school, and Bible study are all good ways of strengthening the church body and helping it grow. As you participate, you grow individually, and as the members participate, the church gets stronger as a whole. The working category is where followers of Jesus Christ motivated by love should care for Jesus by caring for those who are not followers, as well as followers of Jesus Christ as we talked about previously. There are many examples, but I'll give you one. That Sunday school teacher is feeding the people in the group. The teacher themselves is working to strengthen the students so they are stronger to carry out their ministries. Another way to look at this is through looking at the Great Commission in Matthew, "Therefore go and make disciples of all nations, baptizing them in the name of the Father and of the Son and of the Holy Spirit." Often times we read this and say or think this is just for missionaries to other countries. The rest of us just need to sit in church and feed/rest. What happens to a human body that only feeds and rests? It gets weak. When we work for Jesus, we are using our Spiritual gifts, opportunities to bring people to salvation and, once saved, help them learn how to live to be more like Jesus. Let's take a look at 1 Corinthians 12:12–27, "Just as a body, though one has many parts all its many parts form one body, so it is with Christ. For we were all baptized by[c] one Spirit so as to form one body—whether Jews or Gentiles, slave or free—and we were all given the one Spirit to drink. Even so the body is not made up of one part, but of many. Now if the foot should say, 'Because I am not a hand, I do not belong to the body,' it would not for that reason stop being part of the body. ¹And if the ear should say, 'Because I am not an eye, I do not belong to the body,' it would not for that reason stop being part of the body. If the whole body were an eye, where would the sense of hearing be? If the whole body were an ear, where would the sense of smell be? But in fact God has placed the parts in the body, every one of them, just as he wanted them to be. If they were all one part, where would the body be? As it is, there are many parts, but one body. The eye cannot say to the hand, 'I don't need you!' And the head cannot say to the feet, 'I don't need you!' On the contrary, those parts of the body that seem to be weaker are indispensable, and the parts that we think are less honorable we treat with special honor. And the parts that are unpresentable are treated with special modesty, while our presentable parts need no special treatment. But God has put the body together, giving greater honor to the parts that lacked it, so that there should be no division in the body, but that its parts should have equal concern for each other. If one part suffers, every part suffers with it; if one part is honored, every part rejoices with it. Now you are the body of Christ, and each one of you is a part of it." Often times we give honor to the pastor above say the person that sets up the chairs. God says one may be more up front and famous, but both are needed. I'll give you an example. I was part of a ministry where I set up chairs and tables for a dinner to raise money for the pastor to travel and share the Gospel. While a teenage boy and I set up tables and chairs, the people in the kitchen would prepare food. When it was time, the pastor and his wife with others would come and sit at the head table. He would always thank those in the kitchen preparing the food, but not mention of us setting up chairs and tables. I explained to the boy, without us, they would be eating standing up or sitting on the floor. Because of us, they can eat comfortably, which would draw more people who would pay for the meal, which would give more money for the pastor to share the gospel. As we work, we have to keep in mind our actions may be part of a larger chain of events that falls apart if one part breaks down. The out-front gifts are most noticeable, but the behind-the-scene gifts are equally important.

Next I'd like to talk about how we should interact in the church with others. In Acts 42–47, "They devoted themselves to the apostles' teaching and to fellowship, to the breaking of bread and to prayer. Everyone was filled with awe at the many wonders and signs performed by the apostles. All the believers were together and had everything in common. They sold property and possessions to give to anyone who had need. Every day they continued to meet together in the temple courts. They broke bread in their homes and ate together with glad and sincere hearts, praising God and enjoying the favor of all the people. And the Lord added to their number daily those who were being saved." You can see overall a spirit of togetherness. They knew each other, met together, eager to help each other, share with each other, encouraged each other, living as a family, one (worked to eliminate division) and growing. Speaking of growing, a lot of churches strive to become larger. In what we just read, it's hard to imagine they were mega churches. They seem to be smaller to have the characteristic they mentioned. I once attended a church and it was small, and over time, we grew to become a large church. I felt the closeness of the early days were eroded as the church grew. I received in the mail a monthly denomination for our state. In one issue, it gave the number of baptisms and number of members for each church in the state. It was true the larger churches had more baptisms, but when you divide the number of baptisms per member, then the story is different. It shows smaller churches (around two hundred members) more effectively draw people to God. So don't feel bad if you belong to a small church. It has its advantages. If you belong to a large church, you have to work harder at being outward focused and working rather than just feeding and resting. In summary, to be first, remember these things as you are part of the church:

1. There is one global church and each local church should work together.
2. There is one leader, Jesus Christ, and one message the gospel and a collection of followers.
3. Churches care motivated by love for Jesus and all people. We're Jesus's arms, legs, hands, and feet.
4. Church activities a balance of work/rest.
5. All followers called to execute the Great Commission.
6. Know/use the spiritual gifts assigned to you whether they be out-front or behind-the-scene gifts.
7. Local churches should be rightsized and operate like a family.

Next Step: Reflection, Application, and Action

Not at all — 0
Slightly — 2
Some — 4
Much — 6
Very Much — 8
Perfect =Jesus — 10

Ask God to reveal where you are, what to do next, and to help you (five or below should take action).

Priority	Basic Question	Statement	Definition/Detail	Rating	Action to Improve	New Rating	Difference in Rating
God First		I go to church regularly.					
		I am involved in a ministry regularly.	The ministry I'm involved with, I am confident God has assigned me to it.				

CHAPTER 9

PAUL, THIS IS YOUR LIFE

There was a TV show in the late '50s to early '60s and they tried to revive it in the '80s. It was called *This Is Your Life*. They would surprise guests and have friends and relatives come on and talk about the guest. The title of this chapter is "Paul, This Is Your Life." We're going to study his life and then see how he grew to be more like Jesus Christ over four periods of his life. Before he was a Christian, when he became a Christian, as a maturing Christian, and then toward his death. First I'd like to give you some overall highlights:

Early Life
Born in Tarsus
Jew
Roman citizen
Father was a Pharisee

Life as a Pharisee
Studied under Gamaliel, most prestigious teacher
Was present at Stephen's stoning; held the coats
Got permission to hunt down and arrest Christians

Early Life as a Christian
Met Jesus on the road to Damascus and became a Christian
Hid in Arabia

Maturing Christian
Preached boldly in Jerusalem
Went on three missionary journeys, each one longer than the last.
Dispute about John Mark leaving the second missionary trip. Paul upset.
Wrote fourteen books to the churches and individuals after the first missionary journey.

Toward His Death
Invited John Mark on third missionary journey
Arrested in Jerusalem
Sent to Rome
Wrote to Philemon to accept back his runaway slave
Wrote two books to Timothy and one to Titus as a mentor
He preached in Rome

In the final book before his death, he wrote 2 Timothy 4:6–8, "For I am already being poured out like a drink offering, and the time for my departure is near. I have fought the good fight, I have finished the race, I have kept the faith. Now there is in store for me the crown of righteousness, which the Lord, the righteous Judge, will award to me on that day—and not only to me, but also to all who have longed for his appearing."

Emperor Nero blames the fires in Rome on Christians. Paul is beheaded at age sixty-one.

GOD'S MESSAGE TO MEN

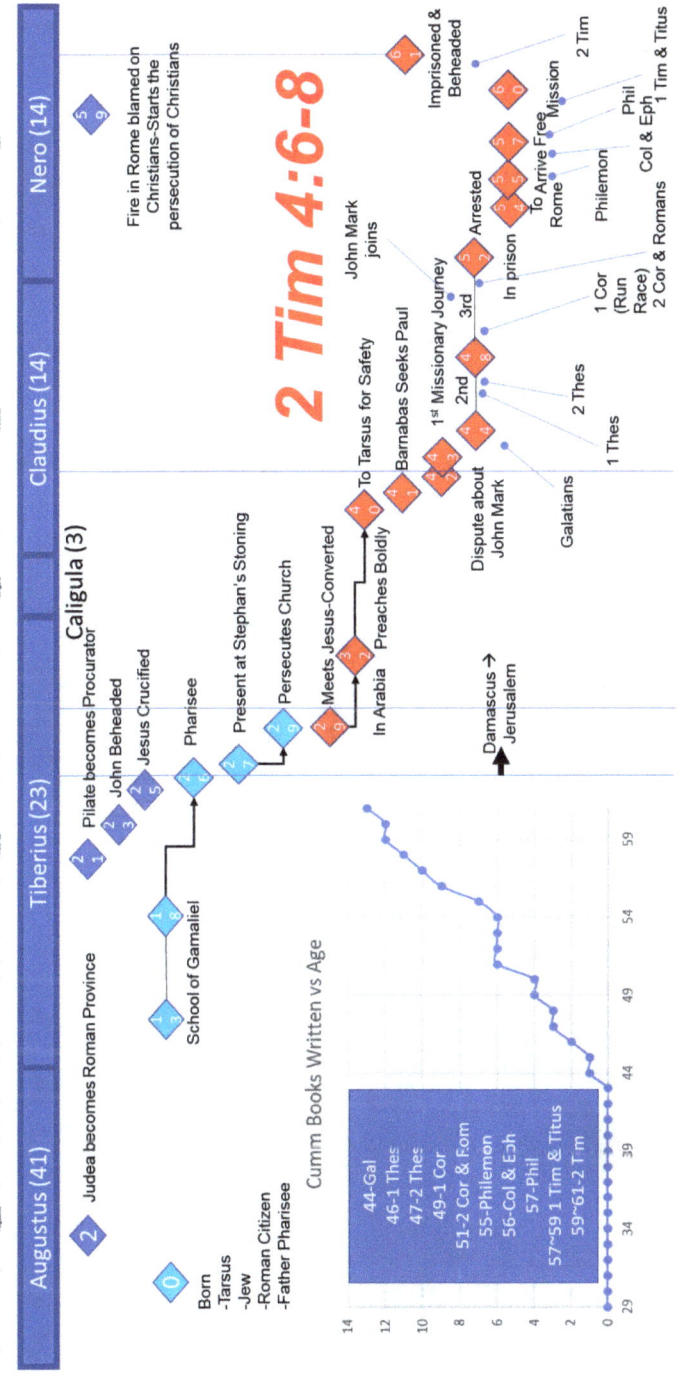

In the next illustration are the maps of Paul's three missionary journeys and trip to Rome.

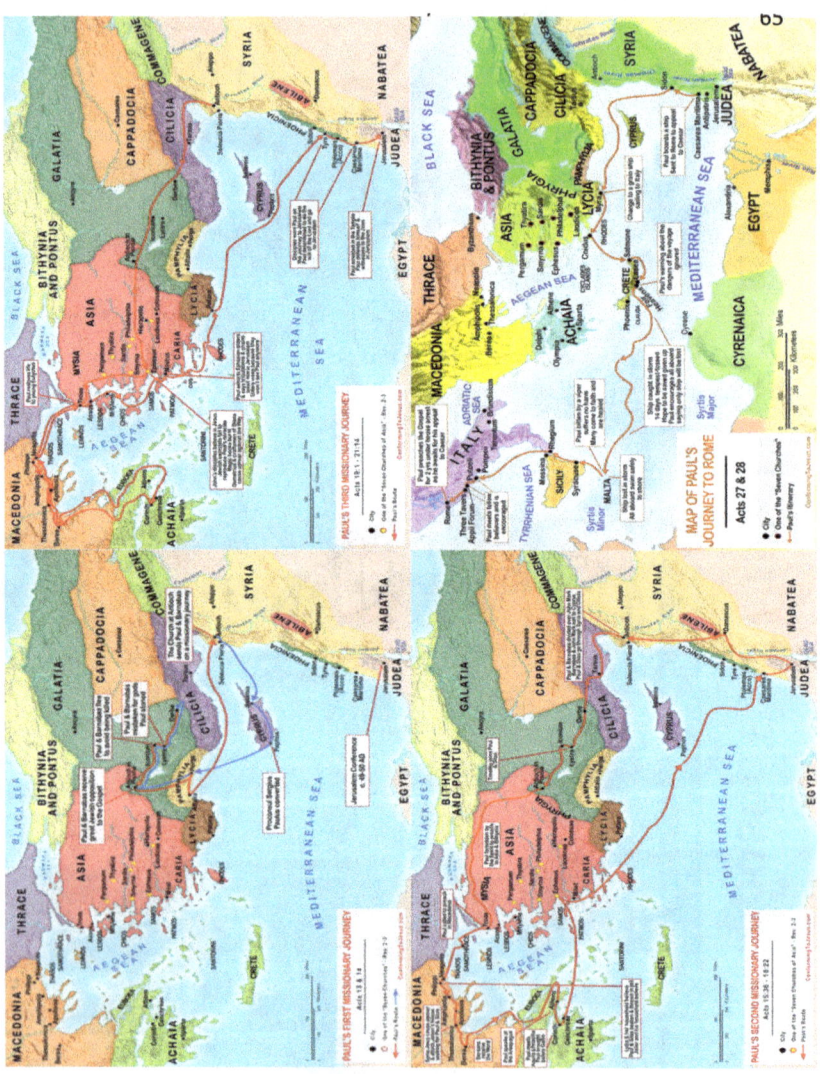

GOD'S MESSAGE TO MEN

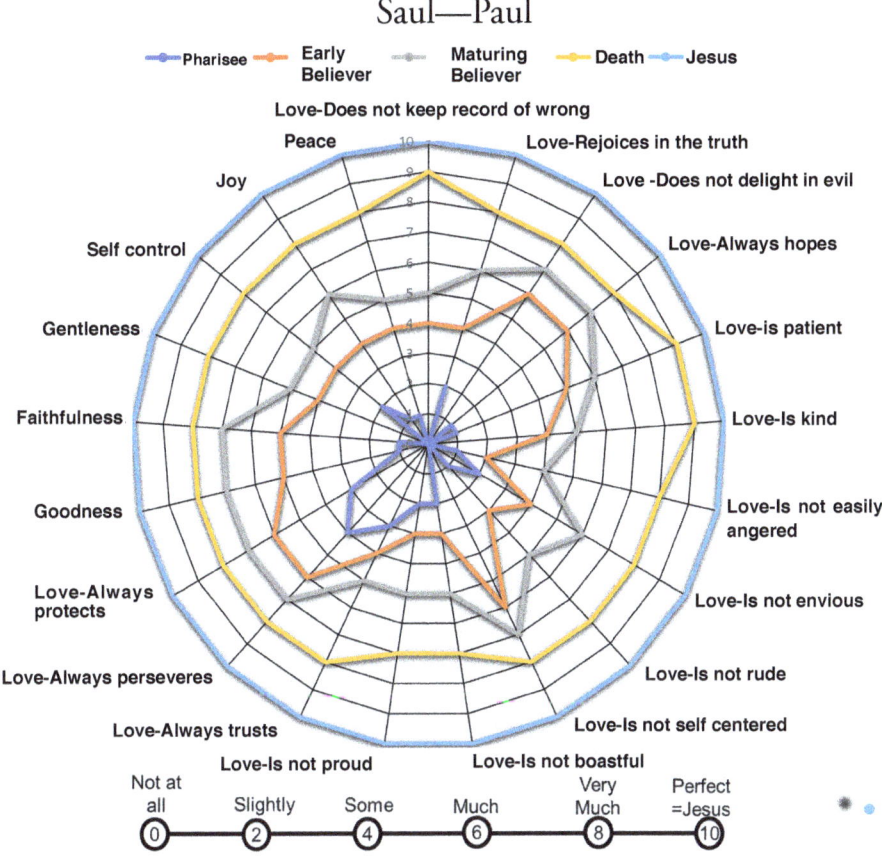

I rated Paul on the 0–10 Scale above on the Love Chapter and Fruit of the Spirit which gives Jesus's characteristics. You may want to do this on your own and may come up with different results. The conclusions I found is the biggest change is from being a Pharisee to a Christian. Immediately, Paul moves closer to being like Christ. Then after becoming a Christian, he grows in the area of Not Keeping Record of Wrongs, Patience, Kindness, and Not Easily Angered. He grew in his forgiveness of John Mark and his compassion toward Philemon's slave. The overall conclusion is great men in the Bible didn't start out that way. Over time, God developed them to be like Jesus. God will do the same for us. Next there is an opportunity to see how you've grown and what action can you take to be more like Christ

Next Step: Reflection, Application, and Action

Ask God to reveal where you are, what to do next, and to help you (five or below should take action).

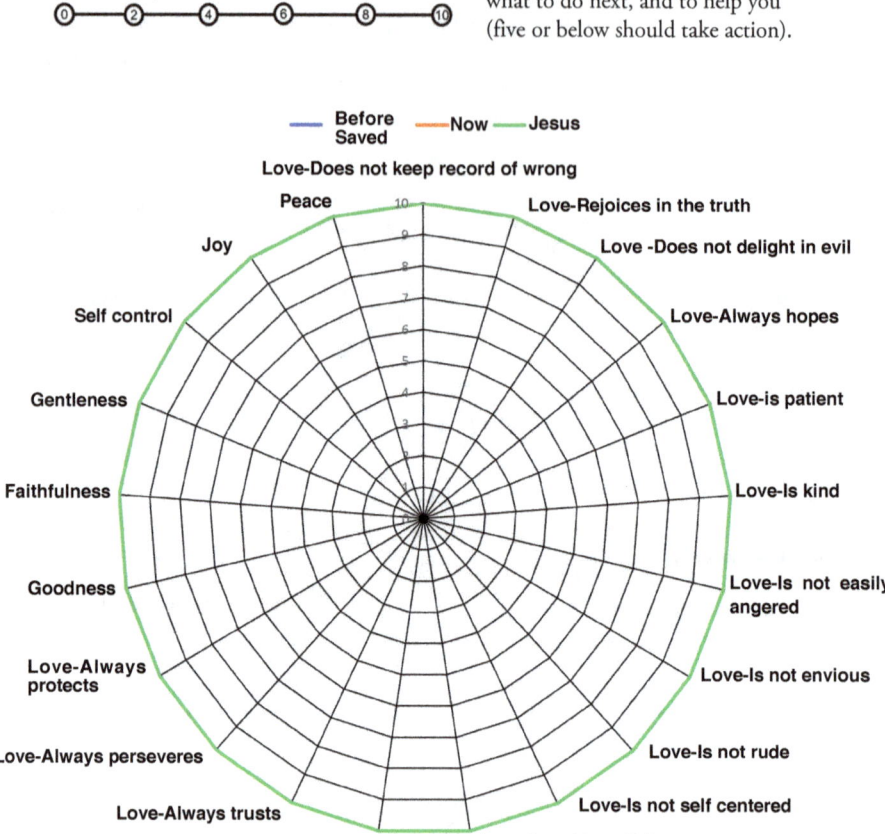

Attributes of Jesus He wants us to have	Definition
Love: Does not keep record of wrong	Forgives and forgets. Overlooks most offenses.
Love: Rejoices in the truth	Celebrates or feels good or encourages others obeying Jesus (the truth).
Love: Does not delight in evil	Does not celebrate or feel good when something bad happens to others or they sin.

GOD'S MESSAGE TO MEN

Attributes of Jesus He wants us to have	Definition
Love: Always hopes	Always has an expectation and desire for good things to happen to others.
Love: Is patient	Able to accept or tolerate delays, problems, or suffering without becoming annoyed or anxious.
Love: Is kind	Having or showing a friendly, generous, and considerate nature.
Love: Is not easily angered	Does not have a quick temper.
Love: Is not envious	Is not jealous, covetous, and resentful.
Love: Is not rude	Is not offensively impolite or ill-mannered.
Love: Is not self-centered	Is not preoccupied with oneself and one's affairs.
Love: Is not boastful	Is not showing excessive pride and self-satisfaction in one's achievements, possessions, or abilities.
Love: Is not proud	Is not having or showing a high or excessively high opinion of oneself or one's importance.
Love: Always trusts	Always has firm belief in the reliability, truth, ability, or strength of others.
Love: Always perseveres	Always continue in a course of action even in the face of difficulty or with little or no prospect of success.
Love: Always protects	Always keep others safe from harm or injury.
Goodness	What we do and say are good and right.
Faithfulness	Trust and loyal on Christ for salvation, believe in the truth/promises of God, and actions match these beliefs.
Gentleness	Humility and thankfulness toward God, and polite, restrained behavior toward others.
Self-control	Choosing to give up trying to control things on our own, surrendering to God for help.
Joy	Choosing to respond to life's difficult situations with inner contentment and satisfaction.

JOSEPH GIAMMARCO

Next Step: Reflection, Application, and Action

Not at all — 0
Slightly — 2
Some — 4
Much — 6
Very Much — 8
Perfect =Jesus — 10

Ask God to reveal where you are, what to do next, and to help you (five or below should take action).

Priority	Basic Question	Statement	Definition/ Detail	Rating	Action to Improve	New Rating	Difference in Rating
God First	Is the Holy Spirit developing you to be like Jesus?	Love: Does not keep record of wrong	Forgives and forgets. Overlooks most offenses.				
		Love: Rejoices in the truth	Celebrates or feels good or encourages others obeying Jesus (the truth).				
		Love: Does not delight in evil	Does not celebrate or feel good when something bad happens to others or they sin.				
		Love: Always hopes	Always has an expectation and desire for good things to happen to others.				
		Love: Is patient	Able to accept or tolerate delays, problems, or suffering without becoming annoyed or anxious.				

GOD'S MESSAGE TO MEN

Priority	Basic Question	Statement	Definition/ Detail	Rating	Action to Improve	New Rating	Difference in Rating
		Love: Is kind	Having or showing a friendly, generous, and considerate nature.				
		Love: Is not easily angered	Does not have a quick temper.				
		Love: Is not envious	Is not jealous, covetous, and resentful.				
		Love: Is not rude	Is not offensively impolite or ill-mannered.				
		Love: Is not self-centered	Is not preoccupied with oneself and one's affairs.				
		Love: Is not boastful	Is not showing excessive pride and self-satisfaction in one's achievements, possessions, or abilities.				
		Love: Is not proud	Is not having or showing a high or excessively high opinion of oneself or one's importance.				

Next Step: Reflection, Application, and Action

Not at all (0) — Slightly (2) — Some (4) — Much (6) — Very Much (8) — Perfect =Jesus (10)

Ask God to reveal where you are, what to do next, and to help you (five or below should take action).

Priority	Basic Question	Statement	Definition/Detail	Rating	Action to Improve	New Rating	Difference in Rating
First: God	Is the Holy Spirit developing you to be like Jesus?	Love: Always trusts	Always has firm belief in the reliability, truth, ability, or strength of others.				
		Love- Always perseveres	Always continues in a course of action even in the face of difficulty or with little or no prospect of success.				
		Love: Always protects	Always keeps others safe from harm or injury.				
		Goodness	What we do and say are good and right.				
		Faithfulness	Trust and loyal to Christ for salvation, believe in the truth/promises of God, and actions match these beliefs.				

GOD'S MESSAGE TO MEN

Priority	Basic Question	Statement	Definition/Detail	Rating	Action to Improve	New Rating	Difference in Rating
		Gentleness	Humility and thankfulness toward God, and polite, restrained behavior toward others.				
		Self-control	Choosing to give up trying to control things on our own, surrendering to God for help.				
		Joy	Choosing to respond to life's difficult situations with inner contentment and satisfaction				
		Peace	A state of rest, completeness, or wholeness and not worry because you see things as God sees them.				

CHAPTER 10

TOP OF THE LEADERBOARD

So far, even though the book is titled *God's Message to Men*, much of this book is applicable to women as well. In this next chapter, we are going to talk about leadership, which women have a role in. However, I'm going to focus on men since many times especially in the church and family, there can be an absence of leadership. Women are filling in where the men should be taking the lead. With that said, the title of this chapter is "Top of the Leaderboard." Many compete, but only one finishes at the top of the leaderboard. This chapter, we are going to talk about how to get to the top of God's leaderboard. There are five keys: mandate, motive, mind, method, mission.

Mandate

Ephesians 5:23 says, "For the husband is the head of the wife as Christ is the head of the church, his body, of which he is the Savior." Gen 1:28b–30 says, "Rule over the fish in the sea and the birds in the sky and over every living creature that moves on the ground." These two verses tell us we are to be leaders in our homes, in our workplaces, and in our communities. This can be a sobering thought for us because we don't choose, but are chosen by God. Sometimes, we can be like Moses at the burning bush, arguing with God to pick someone else because we're not interested, able, or qualified. It doesn't matter what we say or do, and even if we run away like Jonah did in the end, we can't escape what God had mandated for us. We're reminded at restaurants. They assume we are the leader when they give us the check. I know the world is changing, but right now, what is the world like today and how are we men doing as a whole; 84 percent of governors, 76 percent of senators, and 63 percent of representatives are men. Obviously, our government is men dominated, but it seems we lack leadership since problems are not solved in the spirit of teamwork by either parties. In our families, 50 percent of marriages end in divorce; 84 percent of those families are led by single mothers. The consequences of these broken homes without fathers are devastating. Also, 93 percent of prisoners today are men. In his book, *The Power of a Father's Blessing*, Bill Glass said, "The FBI studied the 17 kids that have shot their classmates in little towns like Paducah, Kentucky; Pearl, Mississippi; and Littleton, Colorado. All 17 shooters had only one thing in common. They had a father problem. I see it so much; it's just unbelievable. There's something about it when a man doesn't get along with his father. It makes him mean; it makes him dangerous; it makes him angry."

Studies show daughters will tend to be attracted to men like their fathers. How you love your wife will strongly influence how your daughter will be loved by another. What a sobering thought! Even in the Bible, the good kings had good sons three times more than bad kings did. And these sons whether good or bad led after them. Even though women are contributing more to the family, income is made up typically 70 percent by the husband. This indicates the provision for our families largely depends on us and, while I'm at it, gives us chances to lead in our workplace. If done right, we can kill two birds with one stone by providing for our families and positively influencing others. Interestingly as a consequence for their sin, God tells Adam he will struggle to work to provide for his family, and to Eve, she will be led by Adam. Thanks to Adam and Eve, we men inherit not only their sin nature, but these difficult assignments as well. Thousands of years later, not much has changed.

Regarding spiritual impact studies show two-thirds of children will have an active church life if only their father regularly goes to church. Whereas, if the father never attends church, but the mother regularly does, only one-third of the children as adults will have an active church life. Well, I hope I haven't scared you off yet, but have hopefully convinced you whether you like it or not, we have been assigned a great responsibility and there is a great need for men today to lead in our homes, in our workplace, and in our community today. The first step to be in top of God's leaderboard is to gladly accept the assignment. As my friend Michael who hosts our Bible study says when someone starts to grumble, that's why we were given the broad shoulders!

Motive

Now that we have accepted our assignment, what's next? As a leader, I believe it's as important to know why you're doing something as what's your doing, i.e., the motive behind your action makes all the difference in the world. Jesus said in John 3:16, "God so loved the world that he gave his one and only Son, that whoever believes in him shall not perish but have eternal life." The first part "loved the world" was God's motive behind sending His Son to earth to die for us. He could have said because he wanted to be famous or popular, or show off His power, or so everyone would like God or say He's great, or to become rich and famous. When asked for the two greatest commandments, Jesus answered, "Love God and love people." The motive behind our actions as leaders has to be love for God and others. Everything else is a by-product and not the aim. One way to check your motive is to ask why, why, why; if it finally doesn't arrive back at love of God and others, you need to change your approach!

Mind

When I think of mind, I think of wisdom. Where does a Godly leader get his wisdom from to lead?

Know the Bible

In Deuteronomy 17:18–20, "When he takes the throne of his kingdom, he is to write for himself on a scroll a copy of this law, taken from that of the Levitical priests. It is to be with him, and he is to read it all the days of his life so that he may learn to revere the Lord his God and follow carefully all the words of this law and these decrees and not consider himself better than his fellow Israelites and turn from the law to the right or to the left. Then he and his descendants will reign a long time over his kingdom in Israel." Kings are required to know the Bible. Josiah thought he was doing right, but when he encountered God's word, he realized he was headed for disaster. He took urgent action to change.

Be Strong and Courageous

Joshua 1:6–9 says, "Be strong and courageous, because you will lead these people to inherit the land I swore to their ancestors to give them. Be strong and very courageous. Be careful to obey all the law my servant Moses gave you; do not turn from it to the right or to the left, that you may be successful wherever you go. Keep this Book of the Law always on your lips; meditate on it day and night, so that you may be careful to do everything written in it. Then you will be prosperous and successful. Have I not commanded you? Be strong and courageous. Do not be afraid; do not be discouraged, for the Lord your God will be with you wherever you go." First Kings 2:1–4 says, "When the time drew near for David to die, he gave a charge to Solomon his son. 'I am about to go the way of all the earth,' he said. 'So be strong, act like a man, and observe what the Lord your God requires: Walk in obedience to him, and keep his decrees and commands, his laws and regulations, as written in the Law of Moses.

Do this so that you may prosper in all you do and wherever you go and that the Lord may keep his promise to me: 'If your descendants watch how they live, and if they walk faithfully before me with all their heart and soul, you will never fail to have a successor on the throne of Israel.'"

Have Discernment from God

First Kings 3:5–15 says, "At Gibeon the Lord appeared to Solomon during the night in a dream, and God said, 'Ask for whatever you want me to give you.' Solomon answered, 'You have shown great kindness to your servant, my father David, because he was faithful to you and righteous and upright in heart. You have continued this great kindness to him and have given him a son to sit on his throne this very day. Now, Lord my God, you have made your servant king in place of my father David. But I am only a little child and do not know how to carry out my duties. Your servant is here among the people you have chosen, a great people, too numerous to count or number. So give your servant a discerning heart to govern your people and to distinguish between right and wrong. For who is able to govern this great people of yours?' The Lord was pleased that Solomon had asked for this. So God said to him, 'Since you have asked for this and not for long life or wealth for yourself, nor have asked for the death of your enemies but for discernment in administering justice, I will do what you have asked. I will give you a wise and discerning heart, so that there will never have been anyone like you, nor will there ever be. Moreover, I will give you what you have not asked for—both wealth and honor—so that in your lifetime you will have no equal among kings. And if you walk in obedience to me and keep my decrees and commands as David your father did, I will give you a long life.' Then Solomon awoke—and he realized it had been a dream."

Ask, Seek, and Knock

Matthew 7:7–11 says, "Ask and it will be given to you; seek and you will find; knock and the door will be opened to you. For everyone who asks receives; the one who seeks finds; and to the one who knocks, the door will be opened. Which of you, if your son asks for bread, will give him a stone? Or if he asks for a fish, will give him a snake? If you, then, though you are evil, know how to give good gifts to your children, how much more will your Father in heaven give good gifts to those who ask him!"

Lamp to Feet/Light for Path

Psalms 119:105 says, "Your word is a lamp for my feet, a light on my path."

Wisdom: James 1:5–8 says, "If any of you lacks wisdom, you should ask God, who gives generously to all without finding fault, and it will be given to you. But when you ask, you must believe and not doubt, because the one who doubts is like a wave of the sea, blown and tossed by the wind. That person should not expect to receive anything from the Lord. Such a person is double-minded and unstable in all they do."

Psalms 1:1–3 says, "Blessed is the one who does not walk in step with the wicked or stand in the way that sinners take or sit in the company of mockers, but whose delight is in the law of the Lord, and who meditates on his law day and night. That person is like a tree planted by streams of water, which yields its fruit in season and whose leaf does not wither whatever they do prospers."

Faith without Works: James 2:14–25 says, "What good is it, my brothers and sisters, if someone claims to have faith but has no deeds? Can such faith save them? Suppose a brother or a sister is without clothes and daily food. If one of you says to them, 'Go in peace; keep warm and well fed,' but does nothing about their physical needs, what good is it? In the same way, faith by itself, if it is not accompanied by action, is dead. But someone will say, 'You have faith; I have deeds.' Show me your faith without deeds, and I will show you my faith by my deeds. You believe that there is one God. Good! Even the demons believe that—and shudder. You foolish person, do you want evidence that faith without deeds is useless[a]? Was not our father Abraham considered righteous for what he did when he offered his son Isaac on the altar? You see that his faith and his actions were working together, and his faith was made complete by what he did. And the scripture was fulfilled that says, 'Abraham believed God, and it was credited to him as righteousness,'[b] and he was called God's friend. You see that a person is considered righteous by what they do and not by faith alone."

Psalms 119:105 says, "Your word is a lamp for my feet, a light on my path."

Wisdom Comes from God

James 1:5–8 says, "If any of you lacks wisdom, you should ask God, who gives generously to all without finding fault, and it will be given to you. But when you ask, you must believe and not doubt, because the one who doubts is like a wave of the sea, blown and tossed by the wind. That person should not expect to receive anything from the Lord. Such a person is double-minded and unstable in all they do."

Read/Meditate Bible

Psalms 1:1–3 says, "Blessed is the one who does not walk in step with the wicked or stand in the way that sinners take or sit in the company of mockers, but whose delight is in the law of the Lord, and who meditates on his law day and night. That person is like a tree planted by streams of water, which yields its fruit in season and whose leaf does not wither whatever they do prospers."

Action/Belief

Faith without Works: James 2:14–25 says, "What good is it, my brothers and sisters, if someone claims to have faith but has no deeds?

Can such faith save them? Suppose a brother or a sister is without clothes and daily food. If one of you says to them, 'Go in peace; keep warm and well fed,' but does nothing about their physical needs, what good is it? In the same way, faith by itself, if it is not accompanied by action, is dead. But someone will say, 'You have faith; I have deeds.' Show me your faith without deeds, and I will show you my faith by my deeds. You believe that there is one God. Good! Even the demons believe that—and shudder. You foolish person, do you want evidence that faith without deeds is useless[a]? Was not our father Abraham considered righteous for what he did when he offered his son Isaac on the altar? You see that his faith and his actions were working together, and his faith was made complete by what he did. And the scripture was fulfilled that says, 'Abraham believed God, and it was credited to him as righteousness,'[b] and he was called God's friend. You see that a person is considered righteous by what they do and not by faith alone."

In summary, wisdom to lead comes from God and His Word. We just need to ask, believe, and act with courage.

Are you regularly reading your Bible, praying, attending sermons, Sunday school, Bible study, surrounding yourself with Godly people who can give you counsel?

Method

Taking a look from another angle is characteristics (method) of Jesus's leadership.

- Example: being baptized
- Looks at the heart: twelve disciples

Servant: washing feet

- Longsuffering: patient with his disciples
- Had initiative and took action: always on the go, engaging people ultimately going to the cross for them.

- Attacks the problem, not the person: hates the sin, not the sinner
- Sacrifice: death on the cross
- Develop others: sent them out
- God: dependent and obedient, in the Garden praying to God the Father

In summary, we should lead as Jesus leads: others centered and dependent and obedient to God.

Mission
What Is Finally Accomplished

John 15:5–8 says, "I am the vine; you are the branches. If you remain in me and I in you, you will bear much fruit; apart from me you can do nothing. If you do not remain in me, you are like a branch that is thrown away and withers; such branches are picked up, thrown into the fire and burned. If you remain in me and my words remain in you, ask whatever you wish, and it will be done for you. This is to my Father's glory, that you bear much fruit, showing yourselves to be my disciples." Joshua 24:15 says, "But if serving the Lord seems undesirable to you, then choose for yourselves this day whom you will serve, whether the gods your forefathers served beyond the River, or the gods of the Amorites, in whose land you are living. But as for me and my household, we will serve the Lord." Joshua not only led his household spiritually, but his army and nation too. Wherever God gave him opportunity to lead, he led spiritually. John 3:16 says, "God so loved the world that he gave his one and only Son, that whoever believes in him shall not perish but have eternal life." With God's motive of love for people, He took action by coming to earth and dying on the cross and what was accomplished was we have a way to know God and be saved from eternal punishment! Joseph and Daniel were great leaders who went from being prisoners/captives to being elevated to second in command of kings. Beyond being great leaders of earthly things, the real accomplishment of their leadership was to influence kings and kingdoms to turn their hearts to God.

Great commission is every leader's mission to ultimately glorify God and build his kingdom by loving people and inviting them to know God

There are many things to accomplish as leaders, but the highest priority is to produce a spiritual result where God is glorified and people are drawn to God. How well are you leading spiritually and are you harvesting a spiritual result? If not, reconsider your approach. God is depending on men to lead spiritually.

Wrapping up, I hope you strive to be at the top of god's leadership leaderboard. Remember the five Ms:

> Mandate: Gladly accept the opportunities to lead you've been given.
> Motive: Make sure your ultimate motive for your actions are love for God and people.
> Mind: Wisdom to lead comes from God and His Word. We just need to ask, believe, and act with courage.
> Method: We should lead as Jesus leads. Others centered, dependent, and obedient to God.
> Mission: God is depending on men to lead spiritually, which produces a spiritual result where God is glorified and people are drawn to Him.

Where we need help, let's ask God to help you grow in these five areas!

JOSEPH GIAMMARCO

Next Step: Reflection, Application, and Action

Not at all (0) — Slightly (2) — Some (4) — Much (6) — Very Much (8) — Perfect =Jesus (10)

Ask God to reveal where you are, what to do next, and to help you (five or below should take action).

Priority	Basic Question	Statement	Definition/ Detail	Rating	Action to Improve	New Rating	Difference in Rating
God First	What is characteristic of my leadership?	My wisdom to lead comes from God and His Word.	I just need to ask, believe and act with courage.				
		I lead as Jesus leads.	I'm an example.				
			I'm a servant.				
			I'm longsuffering.				
			I take initiative and action.				
			I sacrifice.				
			I develop others.				
			I'm dependent on God.				
			I'm obedient to God.				
		God is depending on me to lead especially spiritually.	I lead spiritually.				

SECTION 2

SECOND PRIORITY IS WIFE

CHAPTER 11

Cinderella

We have just finished the first priority relationship which is with God. I hope you're enjoying the book so far. We now will start the next major section which is the second priority relationship: marriage. This first chapter is titled "Cinderella." It's a story of a girl whose cruel stepmother and sister force her to do all the cleaning in the house, including the cinders from the fireplace. Her clothes are tattered and soiled with ashes, thus the name Cinderella. Meanwhile, the prince is looking for a wife and throws a ball to meet all the single women. Cinderella is forbidden to go by her stepmother because she isn't presentable. With the help of her fairy godmother, she is able to go to the ball in a lovely gown and driven to it by a spectacular horse-drawn coach. The only catch was at the stroke of midnight, the gown, coach, horses, and everything else would return back to what it originally was. For example, her gown would become the tattered soiled dress again. How embarrassing that would be if she was dancing with the prince. Well, she gets her chance to dance with the prince, and he is smitten by Cinderella. Just then, the clock strikes 12, and she rushes off. As she runs, one of her glass slippers falls off. She is sad because her chance was gone and he was sad because she was the only one he liked. The next day, he goes throughout his entire kingdom looking for the woman that fits the glass slipper. When he gets to Cinderella's house, the stepmother tries to prevent Cinderella from meeting the prince, but finally, they meet and the slipper fits! Her gown and coach reappeared at that moment. She goes from soiled tattered dress to spotless gown. They get married, live in a big castle, and live happily ever after. So what does this mean to marriage in a practical basis? This first chapter, I wanted to explain the ultimate purpose of marriage. Some say for safe sex, companionship, raising children, or populating the earth. These are all important, but are not individually the ultimate purpose for marriage. Let's take a look at some scripture. Ephesians 5:22–33 says, "Wives, submit yourselves to your own husbands as you do to the Lord. For the husband is the head of the wife as Christ is the head of the church, his body, of which he is the Savior. Now as the church submits to Christ, so also wives should submit to their husbands in everything. Husbands, love your wives, just as Christ loved the church and gave himself up for her to make her holy, cleansing[a] her by the washing with water through the word, and to present her to himself as a radiant church, without stain or wrinkle or any other blemish, but holy and blameless. In this same way, husbands ought to love their wives as their own bodies. He who loves his wife loves himself. After all, no one ever hated their own body, but they feed and care for their body, just as Christ does the church—for we are members of his body. For this reason a man will leave his father and mother and be united to his wife, and the two will become one flesh.[b] This is a profound mystery—but I am talking about Christ and the church. However, each one of you also must love his wife as he loves himself, and the wife must respect her husband." In these verses, there is two parallels going on. One is Christ and the church and the other is the husband and wife. Since scripture is going back and forth between the two, it stands to reason that one represents the other. So in conclusion, the ultimate purpose of marriage is to model the relationship of Christ and the church. In the illustration below are some patterns from the scripture.

Model the Relationship of Christ and Church

We see that Christ is synonymous with the husband or groom and the church is synonymous with the wife or bride. Christ seeks to be one with His church as we discussed in the previous chapter about the church. In the same way, the husband and wife are to be one. We'll talk more about that in future chapters. The husband is to be the head, yet in a sacrificial, loving way that positively encourages her to be all she can be in Christ as a Christian. The wife in turn submits, respects, praises, and helps her husband. In the scripture, it talks about Jesus preparing his bride through washing, stain removal, wrinkle removal. In the illustration, the bride is in a wedding gown. Most woman dream about what their wedding gown will look like since they were little girls. Some may plan which one or which style they'll have before they even meet the man they will marry. The man, on the other hand, rents a tux for the day. For the woman, the wedding gown not only needs to be the right style, but also needs to be clean, stain and wrinkle free. Many men say when they see their bride to be just when the ceremony starts where she has her gown on, hair down, and makeup, they see the most beautiful woman ever. That's how Christ sees His church. However, that feeling continues past the wedding day. How can we men preserve that feeling about our wives too. We'll talk later about sacrificing, love, and positive encouragement in future chapters. Let me tickle your imagination for a moment. What if she wore that dress every day and you viewed her every day and you see that beautiful woman you saw on your wedding day. I'm not saying literally, but figuratively. You could have photos of her on that day and you could remark, "You were so beautiful that day and every day since." You could introduce her as your bride and not your wife. I suggest these things because men typically look at the wedding as the finish line. Now that I'm married, I can check this off my list and move on to something else like building a career, etc. Men need to see the wedding day as the beginning. Nowhere in scripture was there an end date. Jesus wants to love the church continually and wants men to love their wives continually. So once again, the ultimate purpose of marriage is to model the relationship of Christ and the church. From this model, we'll break down this into specific pieces shown for how to have oneness and things the husband needs to take responsibility for, including turning Cinderella's tattered, soiled gown into a beautiful princess gown fit for a prince.

GOD'S MESSAGE TO MEN

Next Step: Reflection, Application, and Action

Not at all (0) — Slightly (2) — Some (4) — Much (6) — Very Much (8) — Perfect =Jesus (10)

Ask God to reveal where you are, what to do next, and to help you (five or below should take action).

Priority	Basic Question	Statement	Definition/ Detail	Rating	Action to Improve	New Rating	Difference in Rating
Second: Marriage	Does my marriage model the relationship of Christ and church?	Husband behaves like Jesus and wife like the church.	Husband is the head of, sacrifices for, loves, and positively encourages wife to be all she can be in Christ. Wife submits and respects husband.				

CHAPTER 12

WHOLE IN ONE

In the last chapter, we discover the ultimate purpose of marriage is to model the relationship of Christ and the church. It's as if I were watching a play and they announce because of unavailability the part of Jesus will be played by the husband and the part of the church will be played by the bride. In plays, when this happens, there are always understudies who are ready to step in. These would be the husband and bride who would act out the play instead of Jesus and the church. In this chapter titled "Whole in One," we will discuss ways to achieve oneness in marriage. Like in golf, putting the ball in the hole with only one shot can be very difficult even for a professional like Jack Nicklaus. I hope to give you some advice to make it much easier. First, let's revisit in scripture where it talks about marriage. Genesis 2:24 says, "For this reason a man will leave his father and mother and be united to his wife, and they will become one flesh." When one reads this, they typically think of lovemaking and leave and cleave. One encompasses these, but there is a broader definition I want to work from. Oneness is being one in basic values and not sameness. Sameness implies being identical. God made each individual unique, and together, we are whole. Problems occur when one tries to make the other the same. In the illustration below, we see on the left side oneness and on the right sameness. With the left side, the goal is to individually look for ways to fit together, and on the right, they are forcing each other to fit together

Let's talk about some practical ways to do this. First, you can pray and read the Bible together. I recommend Family Life Marriage Bible which has different topics related to marriage and family interspersed with the Bible. Just spend a little bit each day, as I imagine you have a busy life. However, quickly sharing your prayer requests and praying together fosters oneness. By you praying and reading with her helps keep her gown clean, spotless, and without blemish. It also gives you the chance to positively encourage her. She has the chance to praise and help you. Even if you have no time to pray, you can share your requests and pray separately later. At least you are sharing what's going on in your world with each other. Also, ideally find time to read the Bible a little bit each day together. If you need any encouragement refer back to chapters "The 5 Ws and H of Prayer" and "Elephant Sandwich" for ideas to squeeze in prayer and Bible time into your day and to be inspired on the importance of both.

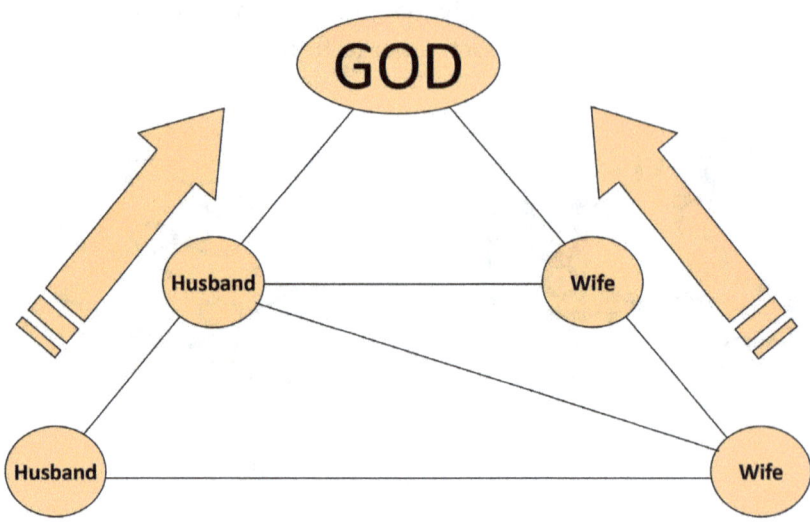

Next, we'll talk about oneness in communication. Communication is the most important thing to master. Whether it's money, parenting, etc., there are always opportunities, concerns, conflict decisions, etc., to come to a solution both the husband and wife can agree to. Even though the husband is head, he is inviting his wife to share her viewpoint. In the following illustration, the cartoon shows the right and wrong way to communicate.

GOD'S MESSAGE TO MEN

93

In the illustration on the previous page, the wrong way appears to want his wife's input; he really just wants her to agree to his. Key phrases like "I think we should do" versus "What do you think I'd like your advice" indicate this difference. In the wrong, the word "problem" is used versus "situation." This word difference comes off as a hard fastball versus an underhanded softball pitch, which create unnecessary tension. In the wrong way, there is combative discussion versus the right way, there is genuine listening and consideration. One of the keys to the right way working is the husband in this case should genuinely listen and only speak to clarify something the wife said that wasn't understood. Repeating back in your own words "what I hear you saying is…is that right?" is a good way to do that. Body language is important too. Leaning toward the listener is a good way to do that. Also, taking notes demonstrates to the speaker they are being heard and understood. Genuinely considering the suggestions conveys the wife is a partner. As you blend your viewpoints together, you come up with the best solution to the concern. Thus achieving oneness. Also, it doesn't have to be the husband who always initiates the discussion, it can be the wife too. This gives both the feeling that their concerns matter and the other is open minded. Think of it in the business world: if the husband is a business owner and he wanted advice from a wife, a consultant business owner, the husband would gladly listen to the advice of the consultant and they would have mutual respect for each other since they are both business owners. Some other tips regarding this technique is to find a time and place you both feel comfortable and at ease discussing. Five minutes before leaving for work may be a little tight and may cause frustration. Also, the sitting alone may not be needed, but if the situation calls for a "let me think about it some, then let's get back together later," you should follow this step. The great thing about this communication technique is it can be used in a variety of ways such as situations like "what do we do about Johnny's poor grades" to "where are we going on our vacation next month?" The more you use this, the more comfortable using it. Instead of fighting and having no resolution, you can come to resolution in a calm manner. This is another way to become one. Next we're going to look at the third idea to promote oneness. On the surface, it may not seem so, but when we think about the puzzle pieces early, it starts to make sense. Below the next page is an illustration the two are trying to find their strengths and weaknesses where they can complement and supplement each other. Thus, making the two weaker puzzle pieces into one stronger one.

Whole in One

To do this, I recommend going to the following personality test from the link below: Search internet for OSPP Four Temperaments Tests

By doing this, you can learn each other's personality and use it to be stronger together. Below is a summary of each personality type. You can use it to further pinpoint specific strengths and weaknesses within your personality type.

Sanguine-Popular	Choleric-Powerful	Melancholy-Perfect	Phlegmatic-Peaceful
Strengths: - Appealing Personality - Talkative, story teller - Life of party - Good sense of humor - Memory for color - Physically holds on to listener - Emotional and demonstrative - Enthusiastic and expressive - Cheerful and bubbling over - Curious - Good on stage - Wide-eyed and innocent - Lives in the present - Changeable disposition - Sincere at heart - Always a child Weaknesses: - Compulsive talker - Exaggerates and elaborates - Dwells on trivia - Can't remember names - Scares others off - Too happy for some - Has restless energy - Egotistical - Blusters and complains - Naïve, gets taken in - Has loud voice and laugh - Controlled by circumstances - Gets angry easily - Seems phony to some - Never grows up	Strengths: - Born leader - Dynamic and active - Compulsive need for change - Must correct wrongs - Strong willed and decisive - Unemotional - Not easily discouraged - Independent and self-sufficient - Exudes confidence - Can run anything Weaknesses: - Bossy - Impatient - Quick tempered - Can't relax - Too impetuous - Enjoys controversy and argument - Won't give up when losing - Comes on too strong - Inflexible - Is not complementary - Dislikes tears and emotions - Is unsympathetic	Strengths: - Deep and thoughtful - Analytical - Serious and purposeful - Genius prone - Talented and creative - Artistic or musical - Philosophical and poetic - Appreciative of beauty - Sensitive to others - Self-sacrificing - Contentious - Idealistic Weaknesses: - Remembers the negative - Moody and depressed - Enjoys being hurt - Has false humility - Off in another world - Low self-image - Has selective hearing - Self-centered - Too introspective - Guilt feelings - Persecution complex - Tends to hypochondria	Strengths: - Low-key personality - Easygoing and relaxed - Calm, cool, and collected - Patient and well balanced - Consistent life - Quiet, but witty - Sympathetic and kind - Keeps emotions hidden - Happily reconciled to life - All-purpose person Weaknesses: - Unenthusiastic - Fearful and worried - Indecisive - Avoids responsibility - Quiet will of iron - Selfish - Too shy and reticent - Too compromising - Self-righteous

GOD'S MESSAGE TO MEN

Sanguine-Popular	Choleric-Powerful	Melancholy-Perfect	Phlegmatic-Peaceful	
- Volunteers for work - Thinks up new activities - Looks great on surface - Creative and colorful - Has energy and enthusiasm - Starts in a flashy way - Inspires others to join - Charms others to work	- Goal oriented - Sees the whole picture - Organizes well - Seeks practical solutions - Moves quickly to action - Delegates work - Insists on production - Makes the goal - Stimulates activity - Thrives on opposition	- Schedule oriented - Perfectionist-high standards - Detail conscious - Persistent and thorough - Orderly and organized - Neat and tidy - Economical - Sees the problems - Finds creative solutions - Needs to finish what he started - Likes charts, graphs, figures, and lists	- Competent and steady - Peaceful and agreeable - Has administrative ability - Mediates problems - Avoids conflict - Good under pressure - Finds the easy way	- Not goal oriented - Lacks self-motivation - Hard to get moving - Resents being pushed - Lazy and careless - Discourages others - Would rather watch
- Would rather talk - Forgets obligations - Doesn't follow through - Confidence fades fast - Undisciplined - Priorities out of order - Decides by feelings - Easily distracted - Wastes time talking	- Little tolerance for mistakes - Doesn't analyze details - Bored by trivia - May make rash decisions - May be rude or tactless - Manipulates people - Demanding of others - End justifies the mean - Work may become his god - Demands loyalty in the ranks			
- Makes friends easily - Loves people - Thrives on compliments - Seems exciting - Envied by others - Doesn't hold grudges - Apologizes quickly - Prevents dull moments - Likes spontaneous activity	- Has little need for friends - Will work for group activity - Will lead and organize - Is usually right - Excels in emergencies	- Makes friends cautiously - Content to stay in background - Avoids causing attention - Faithful and devoted - Will listen to complaints - Can solve other's problems - Deep concern for other people - Moved to tears with compassion - Seeks ideal mate	- Easy to get along with - Pleasant and enjoyable - Inoffensive - Good listener - Dry sense of humor - Enjoys watching people - Has many friends - Has compassion and concern	- Dampens enthusiasm - Stays uninvolved - Is not exciting - Indifferent to plans - Judges others - Sarcastic and teasing - Resists change
- Hates to be alone - Needs to be center stage - Wants to be popular - Looks for credit - Dominates conversation - Interrupts and doesn't listen - Answers for others - Fickle and forgetful - Makes excuses - Repeats stories	- Tends to use people - Dominates others - Decides for others - Knows everything - Can do everything better - Is too independent - Possessive of friend and mate - Can't say "I'm sorry" - May be right, but unpopular	- Lives through others - Insecure socially - Withdrawn and remote - Critical of others - Holds back affection - Dislikes those in opposition - Suspicious of people - Antagonistic and vengeful - Unforgiving - Full of contradictions - Skeptical of compliments		

97

The fourth item is opposite of the first three. Instead of building oneness, it destroys it. Let's look at some scripture. Exodus 20:14 says, "You shall not commit adultery." First Corinthians 6:16 says, "Do you know that he who unites himself with a prostitute is one with her in body? For it is said, 'The two will become one flesh.'" Proverbs 6:32 says, "But a man who commits adultery lacks judgment; whoever does so destroys himself." Matthew 5:27–28 says, "You have heard that it was said, do not commit adultery. But I tell you that anyone who looks at a woman lustfully has already committed adultery with her in his heart."

So what destroys oneness? Unfaithfulness, physically and mentally.

In conclusion, by

1. Praying and reading the Bible together.
2. Applying oneness in communication.
3. Learning each other's personality.
4. Being faithful to your wife (avoiding and running away from temptation), you can achieve oneness in your marriage.

GOD'S MESSAGE TO MEN

Next Step: Reflection, Application, and Action

Not at all (0) — Slightly (2) — Some (4) — Much (6) — Very Much (8) — Perfect =Jesus (10)

Ask God to reveal where you are, what to do next, and to help you (five or below should take action).

Priority	Basic Question	Statement	Definition/ Detail	Rating	Action to Improve	New Rating	Difference in Rating
Second: Marriage	Is there oneness in my marriage?	There is oneness in values in my marriage.					
		We seek God's will together thru prayer and reading the Bible.					
		We practice oneness in communication and to resolve issues					
		We learned our personality types and are using that knowledge to become one.	Understand where strengths and weaknesses compliment and supplement each other.				
		I'm faithful physically and mentally.					

CHAPTER 13

ANGELO

In this chapter, we will discuss where God created a helper for the man. I've titled this chapter "Angelo" after Angelo Argea. According to Wikipedia, Angelo Argea was best known as the caddie for Jack Nicklaus

He and Nicklaus first met at the Palm Springs Golf Classic in 1963, when Argea signed up to caddie for him. Argea continued to caddie for Nicklaus for over twenty years. Argea was easily recognizable by his gray afro. Of Argea, Nicklaus has remarked, "Essentially, he has been retired since he was twenty-one." A golfer once noticed that Argea didn't read greens, step off the yardage, or select clubs, so he asked Argea, "What exactly do you do for Jack?" Argea replied, "He asked me to do two things. When he's not playing well, one, remind him that he's the best golfer out there. And two, that there's plenty of holes left."

"Angelo was known for his gray afro, but he should also be known for being an excellent caddie," Nicklaus said.

He was inducted into the PCA Worldwide Caddie Hall of Fame in 1999.

The primary verses that talk about a helper for Adam is Genesis 2:20–22, "But for Adam no suitable helper was found. So the Lord God caused the man to fall into a deep sleep; and while he was sleeping, he took one of the man's ribs[g] and then closed up the place with flesh. Then the Lord God made a woman from the rib[h] he had taken out of the man, and he brought her to the man."

In the illustration, we see God taking out a rib from the man to create the woman. Why a rib and not a piece of the skull or foot? These would symbolize the woman is over the man or the man steps on the woman. Whereas the rib shows she is by his side, she guards his vital organs like his heart, and she can give the man another or woman's point of view.

A great example is about Nabel, Abigail, and David.

First Samuel 25:2–35 says, "A certain man in Maon, who had property there at Carmel, was very wealthy. He had a thousand goats and three thousand sheep, which he was shearing in Carmel. His name was Nabal and his wife's name was Abigail. She was an intelligent and beautiful woman, but her husband was surly and mean in his dealings—he was a Calebite. While David was in the wilderness, he heard that Nabal was shearing sheep. So he sent ten young men and said to them, 'Go up to Nabal at Carmel and greet him in my name. Say to him: "Long life to you! Good health to you and your household! And good health to all that is yours! Now I hear that it is sheep-shearing time. When your shepherds were with us, we did not mistreat them, and the whole time they were at Carmel nothing of theirs was missing. Ask your own servants and they will tell you. Therefore be favorable toward my men, since we come at a festive time. Please give your servants and your son David whatever you can find for them." When David's men arrived, they gave Nabal this message in David's name. Then they waited. Nabal answered David's servants, 'Who is this David? Who is this son of Jesse? Many servants are breaking away from their masters these days. Why should I take my bread and water, and the meat I have slaughtered for my shearers, and give it to men coming from who knows where?' David's men turned around and went back. When they arrived, they reported every word. David said to his men, 'Each of you strap on your sword!' So they did, and David strapped his on as well. About four hundred men went up with David, while two hundred stayed with the supplies. One of the servants told Abigail, Nabal's wife, 'David sent messengers from the wilderness to give our master his greetings, but he hurled insults at them. Yet these men were very good to us. They did not mistreat us, and the whole time we were out in the fields near them nothing was missing. Night and day they were a wall around us the whole time we were herding our sheep near them. Now think it over and see what you can do, because disaster is hanging over our master and his whole household. He is such a wicked man that no one can talk to him.' Abigail acted quickly. She took two hundred loaves of bread, two skins of wine, five dressed sheep, five seahs[b] of roasted grain, a hundred cakes of raisins and two hundred cakes of pressed figs, and loaded them on donkeys. Then she told her servants, 'Go on ahead; I'll follow you.' But she did not tell her husband Nabal. As she came riding her donkey into a mountain ravine, there were David and his men descending toward her, and she met them. David had just said, 'It's been useless—all my watching over this fellow's property in the wilderness so that nothing of his was missing. He has paid me back evil for good. May God deal with David,[c] be it ever so severely, if by morning I leave alive one male of all who belong to him!' When Abigail saw David, she quickly got off her donkey and bowed down before David with her face to the ground. She fell at his feet and said: 'Pardon your servant, my lord, and let me speak to you; hear what your servant has to say. Please pay no attention, my lord, to that wicked man Nabal. He is just like his name—his name means Fool, and folly goes with him. And as for me, your servant, I did not see the men my lord sent. And now, my lord, as surely as the Lord your God lives and as you live, since the Lord has kept you from bloodshed and from avenging yourself with your own hands, may your enemies and all who are intent on harming my lord be like Nabal. And let this gift, which your servant has brought to my lord, be given to the men who follow you. Please forgive your servant's presumption. The Lord your God will certainly make a lasting dynasty for my lord, because you fight the Lord's battles, and no wrongdoing will be found in you as long as you live. Even though someone is pursuing you to take your life, the life of my lord will be bound securely in the bundle of the living by the Lord your God, but the lives of your enemies he will hurl away as from the pocket of a sling. When the Lord has fulfilled for my lord every good thing he promised concerning him and has appointed him ruler over Israel, my lord will not have on his conscience the staggering burden of needless bloodshed or of having avenged himself. And when the Lord your God has brought my lord success, remember your servant.' David said to Abigail, 'Praise be to the Lord, the God of Israel, who has sent you today to meet me. May you be blessed for your good judgment and for keeping me from bloodshed this day and from avenging myself with my own hands. Otherwise, as surely as the Lord, the God of Israel, lives, who has kept me from harming you, if you had not come quickly to meet me, not one male belonging to Nabal would have been left alive by daybreak.' Then David accepted from her hand what she had brought him and said, 'Go home in peace. I have heard your words and granted your request.'"

Both Nabal and David took the typical men response which was insults and fighting which would have resulted in lots of people killed. Abigail appealed to David's becoming king some day and his obedience to God to turn away his wrath. In my experience, women typically don't react violently. So Abigail was giving the woman's point of view. She calmed David down to where he realized what that his action would not only hurt him, but many innocent people. Other ways a wife can help you is you can delegate responsibility to her, help make decisions and advice (see oneness in communication), give you another viewpoint (see Abigail). Men tend to be accomplishment experts and women tend to be relationship experts. So if the issue being discussed is relationship oriented, the women's point of view can be especially helpful. Nabal and David were focusing on stuff whereas Abigail was focusing on David's relationship with God. There are other ways your wife can help is by sharing the load, supplement or complement your talents and abilities (see knowing your personality types), and cheering you on! Going back to Angelo and Jack, it was written a golfer once noticed that Argea didn't read greens, step off the yardage, or select clubs, so he asked Argea, "What exactly do you do for Jack?"

Argea replied, "He asked me to do two things. When he's not playing well, one, remind him that he's the best golfer out there. And two, that there's plenty of holes left."

"Angelo was known for his gray afro, but he should also be known for being an excellent caddie," Nicklaus said.

The greatest golfer ever told us that Angelo was an excellent caddy and the main thing he did for Jack was cheer him on. What a blessing it is to have a wife who will cheer you on related to being a Godly man, a husband, a father, an employee, etc. In summary, "Thank God for your wife. Value her as a gift from God. Utilize her abilities to help you lead."

GOD'S MESSAGE TO MEN

Next Step: Reflection, Application, and Action

Not at all (0) — Slightly (2) — Some (4) — Much (6) — Very Much (8) — Perfect =Jesus (10)

Ask God to reveal where you are, what to do next, and to help you (five or below should take action).

Priority	Basic Question	Statement	Definition/ Detail	Rating	Action to Improve	New Rating	Difference in Rating
Second: Marriage	I appropriately utilize my wife as a helpmate.	I treat her as my partner.					
		I value her viewpoint.	Guards my mind and heart.				
		I can delegate responsibility to her.					
		She helps me make decisions and advices.					
		She gives me a woman's viewpoint.					
		We share the load together.					
		She supplements or complements my talents and abilities.					

CHAPTER 14

LOVE YOUR WIFE

No catchy chapter title since this chapter focuses on the same area as "Paul, This Is Your Life." The difference is you'll be measuring where you are in loving your wife. Let's take a look at a Bible verse: Ephesians 5:25, "Husbands, love your wives, just as Christ loved the church and gave himself up for her." What's interesting about this verse is it seems so obvious that husbands should love their wives. Why is it even written? To unlock the mystery in another verse, it says for wives to respect their husbands. This is not intuitive. You would expect it to say, "Wives, love your husbands." Why love versus respect? Because men desired to be respected and women desired to be loved. Based on that, it makes sense that these verses are in the Bible. Also, these verses are not suggestions; they are commandments and both are unconditional. Often, a husband will not love his wife because she does not respect him and vice versa. Take a look below at the illustration of conditional versus unconditional love.

GOD'S MESSAGE TO MEN

How well are you loving your wife?

Conditional-Wrong **Unconditional-Right**

Seems familiar? Now let's get into measuring where you are in loving your wife.

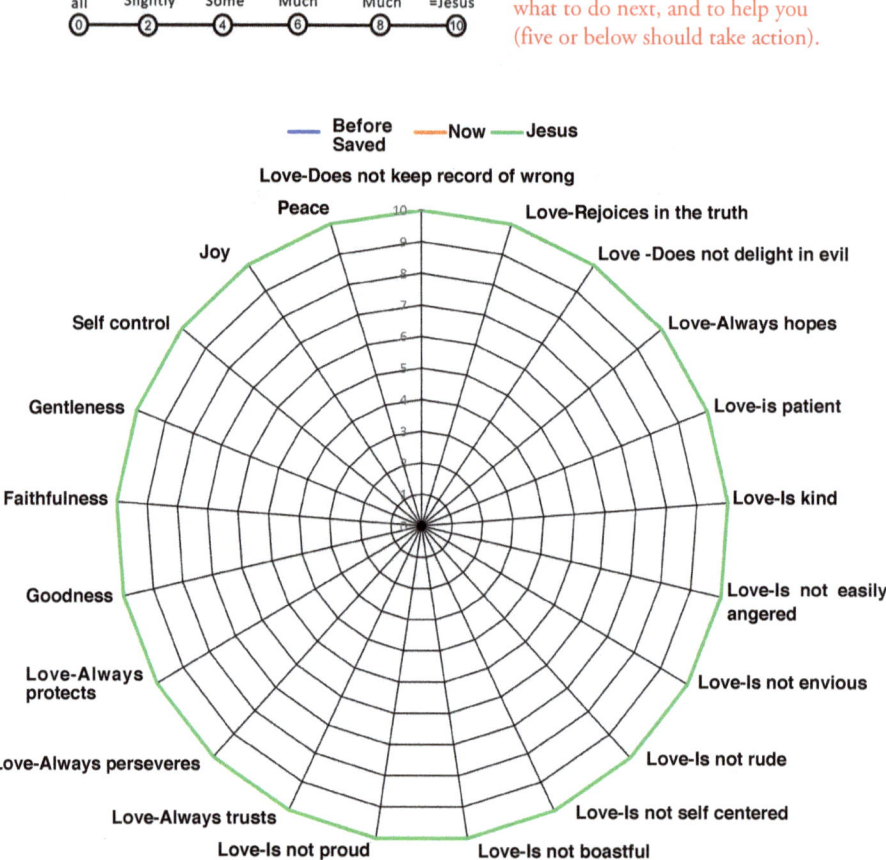

Attributes of Jesus He wants us to have	Definition
Love: Does not keep record of wrong	Forgives and forgets. Overlooks most offenses.
Love: Rejoices in the truth	Celebrates or feels good or encourages others obeying Jesus (the truth).
Love: Does not delight in evil	Does not celebrate or feel good when something bad happens to others or they sin.

Attributes of Jesus He wants us to have	Definition
Love: Always hopes	Always has an expectation and desire for good things to happen to others.
Love: Is patient	Able to accept or tolerate delays, problems, or suffering without becoming annoyed or anxious.
Love: Is kind	Having or showing a friendly, generous, and considerate nature.
Love: Is not easily angered	Does not have a quick temper.
Love: Is not envious	Is not jealous, covetous, and resentful.
Love: Is not rude	Is not offensively impolite or ill-mannered.
Love: Is not self-centered	Is not preoccupied with oneself and one's affairs.
Love: Is not boastful	Is not showing excessive pride and self-satisfaction in one's achievements, possessions, or abilities.
Love: Is not proud	Is not having or showing a high or excessively high opinion of oneself or one's importance.
Love: Always trusts	Always has firm belief in the reliability, truth, ability, or strength of others.
Love: Always perseveres	Always continue in a course of action even in the face of difficulty or with little or no prospect of success.
Love: Always protects	Always keep others safe from harm or injury.
Goodness	What we do and say are good and right.
Faithfulness	Trust and loyal on Christ for salvation, believe in the truth/promises of God, and actions match these beliefs.
Gentleness	Humility and thankfulness toward God, and polite, restrained behavior toward others.
Self-control	Choosing to give up trying to control things on our own, surrendering to God for help.
Joy	Choosing to respond to life's difficult situations with inner contentment and satisfaction.
Peace	A state of rest, completeness, or wholeness and not worry because you see things as God sees them.

Next Step: Reflection, Application, and Action

Rating scale: Not at all (0) — Slightly (2) — Some (4) — Much (6) — Very Much (8) — Perfect =Jesus (10)

Ask God to reveal where you are, what to do next, and to help you (five or below should take action).

Priority	Basic Question	Statement	Definition/Detail	Rating	Action to Improve	New Rating	Difference in Rating
Second: Marriage	Do I love my wife unconditionally?	Love: Does not keep record of wrong	Forgives and forgets. Overlooks most offenses.				
		Love: Rejoices in the truth	Celebrates or feels good or encourages others obeying Jesus (the truth).				
		Love: Does not delight in evil	Does not celebrate or feel good when something bad happens to others or they sin.				
		Love: Always hopes	Always has an expectation and desire for good things to happen to others.				
		Love: Is patient	Able to accept or tolerate delays, problems, or suffering without becoming annoyed or anxious.				

GOD'S MESSAGE TO MEN

Priority	Basic Question	Statement	Definition/Detail	Rating	Action to Improve	New Rating	Difference in Rating
		Love: Is kind	Having or showing a friendly, generous, and considerate nature.				
		Love: Is not easily angered	Does not have a quick temper.				
		Love: Is not envious	Is not jealous, covetous, and resentful.				
		Love: Is not rude	Is not offensively impolite or ill-mannered.				
		Love: Is not self-centered	Is not preoccupied with oneself and one's affairs.				
		Love: Is not boastful	Is not showing excessive pride and self-satisfaction in one's achievements, possessions, or abilities.				
		Love: Is not proud	Is not having or showing a high or excessively high opinion of oneself or one's importance.				

Priority	Basic Question	Statement	Definition/Detail	Rating	Action to Improve	New Rating	Difference in Rating
		Love: Always trusts	Always has firm belief in the reliability, truth, ability, or strength of others.				
		Love: Always perseveres	Always continue in a course of action even in the face of difficulty or with little or no prospect of success.				
		Love: Always protects	Always keep others safe from harm or injury.				
	I practice other tips on marriage.	Don't treat my wife as possession.					
		Don't treat my wife as sex object.					
		Don't love based on being able to bear children.					
		I pray for and encourage my wife.					
		I date my wife regularly.					
		I kiss and hug my wife regularly.					

GOD'S MESSAGE TO MEN

Priority	Basic Question	Statement	Definition/ Detail	Rating	Action to Improve	New Rating	Difference in Rating
		I listen to my wife and don't try to fix things.					
		I leave love notes and texts regularly.					

CHAPTER 15

LOVE LANGUAGES

Once again, no fancy title. Love languages is a concept by Gary Chapman. The theory is people have a love language they prefer spoken or acted on by others. When this happens, the person feels loved and appreciated. These words or actions are spontaneous. The goal is by speaking the love language, you keep that person's love tank full. The love languages and their definitions are the following:

1. Words of affirmation: Saying supportive things to someone.
2. Acts of service: Doing helpful things for someone.
3. Receiving gifts: Giving gifts to someone that tell them you were thinking about them.
4. Quality time: Spending meaningful time with someone.
5. Physical touch: Being close to and touch someone.

Where couples get into trouble is when they're speaking a different language. Usually their own. For example, the husband is cleaning the kitchen because his love language is acts of service; meanwhile, the wife is sitting on the couch waiting to talk to her husband and share their day with each other because her gift is quality time. She's mad because he won't talk to her, and he's mad because she won't help him. The smart husband would drop what he's doing and go share with his wife. Next step is for you to go to the Love Language website in the link below and find out you and your wife's love language and start speaking hers to her.

Link: http://www.5lovelanguages.com/quizzes/couples-quiz/

Next Step: Reflection, Application, and Action

Not at all (0) — Slightly (2) — Some (4) — Much (6) — Very Much (8) — Perfect =Jesus (10)

Ask God to reveal where you are, what to do next, and to help you (five or below should take action).

Priority	Basic Question	Statement	Rating	Action to Improve	New Rating	Difference in Rating
Second: Marriage	Do you know and speak your wife's love language?	Understand your wife's love language and speak it to her.				

CHAPTER 16

MY JOURNEY TO PEACE

This is titled "My Journey to Peace" because it is my journey to peace. About fifteen years ago, my children were still small, I was working happily as a manager and my sister and mom were still alive. Up to that point, I had a temper, but it was concealed behind closed doors where only my wife would see. It was a tamer hurricane with an apology at the end. The first domino to fall was my sister passing away. She had her thyroid gland removed, which then she relied on medication to regulate what the thyroid used to do before. Well, the doctors weren't dialed in yet, and this caused my sister to become depressed and eventually suicidal. Her first attempt was drinking drain cleaner. She wasn't supposed to, but pulled through after one month in Intensive Care. When she was well enough, they put her in a step-down unit. It did not have so many staff and so much equipment. This was further signs she was getting better. In that environment, I told her the Gospel like I did in the chapter "From Famous to Friend." She accepted! So now we are rolling! She attempts suicide, God saves her from death, she accepts Jesus as her Lord and Savior. What's next, sharing her testimony, etc. How exciting! Well, once put back on the medication for depression, she soon became depressed again. In a few weeks, we were back where we were, except she had succeeded this time by standing in front of a train. My brother-in-law was devastated and my mom as well. This meant I had to take the lead to arrange the funeral. I was a mixture of hating God because He pulled the rug out, it seemed, busy with the funeral arrangements and consoling my mom and brother-in-law. Since my sister relinquished the caring for my mom to me, this was added responsibility I would take on. I had no time to grieve. I went to one suicide support group meeting with my brother-in-law and felt like it was a waste of time. After all, I was taught to just be hard as a rock and stuff this down inside. Just like my Hollywood hero John Wayne and my dad would do. It took me two years to dismantle the home care system my sister created, move my mom into an assisted living facility, and sell her house. On top of that, at work, although I'm a manager, I'm assigned another project on top of that. I get a difficult to deal with manager whose work I am assigned. Later, they add another department in between me and top management. After talking directly to top management for nine years, we are in the back seat. Also, HR gets interested in improving conditions for associates and some associates in my department complain about me. HR brings the complaints to the department above me. Meanwhile, I have stuffed even more and noticed my temper is getting shorter. I feel like yelling at the person behind them. In other words, I'm mad at something else. Perhaps something I've tried to keep stuffed is trying to come up. Increasingly, I'm yelling at my spouse in front of my children. One incident was I was sad about my sister and was looking for consolation from my wife, but she was busy decorating for Christmas with the kids. I blew up and asked if is she trying to say she wants a divorce and my younger daughter cried as well. I was having similar incidents with my coworkers too. Then it happens. I get called to a meeting with a top manager about a position they would like me to interview for. Then it happened again. I get a phone call from the doctor at my mom's assisted living who said her heart was beating rapidly and she should be brought to the emergency room. Since she was playing bingo, she resisted going. After I talked to her she agreed to go. It seemed like something minor. The next day, she was in ICU and remained there for a month. I stayed there every day holding out hope as she slowly died of lung issues. I was there the moment she died. Another funeral…more stuffing. After the funeral, it's time to go for my job interview. I flew there as it was in another state. I stayed there for three days, interviewing, checking out private schools, and housing. In the end, I was a good candidate except with small children, it would not be ideal as there was a lot of travel. We both mutually agreed. When I returned and the result came back, my manager called me into a room and told me I was a no-good manager and was being removed. What just happened? I hated coming into work, staying in my area, and talking with my coworkers. More stuffing…more anger! Then came the ordeal with my other son. About four years after this, he decided he was going to drive his grade point down from a 3.7 to a 2.0 by graduation (two years). This situation caused a lot of yelling from us to our son and each other as we couldn't agree how to handle him. The other two kids cried because they didn't like the yelling. And the child ignored any correction. The last incident was with my other son. I was urging him to come see two former Buckeye football players who were playing in the NFL. These players had visited our church several times and we had met them. He wouldn't come. He said no. I said, "Either give me new information or give me your cell phone."

He not only said no, but stood up and said, "If you want it, you have to take it from me."

A shoving match ensued for a few minutes, then I broke it off. He called his mom in tears and she came home. Turns out he was working on a school report and was busy. However, he didn't reveal that to me. Even though we apologized to each other, we became distant as the year wore on. In the next fall, he had his annual physical and the doctor asked him if he had any medical problems since he last saw him. He said he had a panic attack. My son conveyed the incident to him. The doctor reported it to Child Services. They just said, "You may want to get counseling to help you be patient with today's child."

By the end of the year, I came home one night after work and the house was dark, some things have been moved around, and there was a note on the kitchen island saying they had moved out. I spent the night watching *Birdman of Alcatraz* and driving around looking for them. The next morning, I went to church knowing the pastor would be working on his Sunday sermon and told him all about it and asked him to counsel me. He agreed to help me. I'm going to abbreviate counseling me into two activities. With my pastor, we noticed I was harboring unforgiveness in my heart. Maybe because I'm Italian, or I followed my dad's example, or have so much built up inside from being picked on. What my pastor suggested I do was write out what happened to me that I couldn't forgive. Pray to God to forgive me. Believe me when I say I was watering his carpet when I prayed, but didn't shed a tear when I was writing them. We did a few each day until I emptied all twenty-seven of them. After each one, he would ask me if that person knows or still can be reached. If not, he would say leave it in God's hands. If so, I would ask forgiveness to each person personally. That was around half the people. This activity unburdened my shoulders and took a weight off my chest. After that, I did another activity with another therapist who had me examine memories when I was child. I remember my dad didn't ever say "I love you." This memory harmed my self-esteem. After looking at the Saturday morning routine of going to his shop and doing some odd jobs and going to an Italian food store in his pick-up truck with his arm around me definitely showed me he loved me. Once again with me not harboring unforgiveness and relationships in order, my temper shrank and overlooking offenses grew. That's my journey to peace.

SECTION 3

THIRD PRIORITY IS CHILDREN

CHAPTER 17

Doughnut Holes

As we end the chapters on the relation to your wives and move to our relationship to our children, we have a transition chapter I've titled "Doughnut Holes" The reason for this title is that in a doughnut in the center, there is nothing, thus we call it a doughnut hole. Some families approach life as if the hole is filled in. In other words, there is no doughnut hole. So what am I getting at? What I'm talking about is marriage- versus children-centered families. Take a look at the illustration below.

Wrong–Children-Centered Family   Right–Marriage-Centered Family

On the left represents the wrong way, having a child-centered family. And on the right represents the right way, as a marriage-centered family. What's really the difference? In the marriage-centered family, the priority relationship is the parents, better known as the husband and wife. The pitfall of the child-centered family is all the priority of time, activities, etc., is given to the children. The calendar is full and the bank account empty. The husband and wife relationship takes a back seat. As the children grow in number and size, the husband and wife relationship is in a state of neglect. As the children leave the nest, the husband and wife find they don't know how to interact with each other anymore. In the marriage-centered family, the husband and wife keep up on dating, spending long weekends and vacations alone together. They still have fun! When the empty nest comes, they still have each other. So put time in the calendar and money in the budget for activities. Now, I'll leave you with this thought many have said: the best thing for children is for them to know their parents have a strong marriage.

Next Step: Reflection, Application, and Action

Not at all (0) — Slightly (2) — Some (4) — Much (6) — Very Much (8) — Perfect =Jesus (10)

Ask God to reveal where you are, what to do next, and to help you (five or below should take action).

Priority	Basic Question	Statement	Rating	Action to Improve	New Rating	Difference in Rating
Third: Children	Do I have a marriage-centered family?	Parents keeping the marriage relationship higher than the children.				

CHAPTER 18

EYES OF THE LORD

This next chapter is titled "Eyes of the Lord." This is a reference to 1 and 2 Kings and 1 and 2 Chronicles where after each king succeeds the previous king, God summarizes the results of His reign. Here are a couple of examples: 2 Chronicles 20:32 says, "He followed the ways of his father Asa and did not stray from them; he did what was right in the eyes of the Lord." First Kings 16:30 says, "Ahab son of Omri did more evil in the eyes of the Lord than any of those before him." If they were good kings, it would say they did right in the eyes of the Lord, and if they were bad kings, it said they did evil in the eyes of the Lord. In almost all cases, the previous king was the father of the new king. I can imagine the son being groomed by the father to take over being king someday. The son had a bird's-eye view of his father and how he conducted himself as king. Not only that, but in all aspects in his life. Just like your children are watching and seeing how you relate to God, your wife, your children, and your world, do you want them to see right or evil? I'm certain you want them to see right. By studying how God labeled each king, I found three interesting facts:

- Good kings had good sons three times more than bad kings.
- Good kings reigned three times longer than bad kings.

- Thirty-four percent of bad kings did not have sons; they were assassinated.

Generally speaking, good kings produce good sons and bad kings produce bad sons. So as you go about your day and are interacting with the four priority relationships, remember your children are watching and more than likely follow the path you're on. This is not a guarantee, but certainly is a strong influence. In summary, be a godly example. You will influence your children positively by doing right in the eyes of the Lord.

Next Step: Reflection, Application, and Action

Not at all (0) — Slightly (2) — Some (4) — Much (6) — Very Much (8) — Perfect =Jesus (10)

Ask God to reveal where you are, what to do next, and to help you (five or below should take action).

Priority	Basic Question	Statement	Rating	Action to Improve	New Rating	Difference in Rating
Third: Children	Am I a godly example for my children?	I do right in the eyes of the Lord.				

CHAPTER 19

The Flying Wallendas

This next chapter is titled "The Flying Wallendas." According to Wikipedia, Karl Wallenda was a German-American high-wire artist and founder of the Flying Wallendas, a daredevil circus act which performed dangerous stunts, often without a safety net. He was the great-grandfather of current performer Nik Wallenda. I chose this title because we're going to talk about parenting in areas that we need to be balanced which is like a tightrope walk act without a net. Staying perfectly on the tightrope keeps you safe. Leaning toward one side or the other means doom. Karl actually met that doom when, at seventy-three, he was attempting to cross on a wire between two towers without a net.

The first area is obedience versus anger, frustration, and discouragement. It says in Ephesians 6:1, "Children, obey your parents in the Lord, for this is right." Then it goes on to say in Ephesians 6:4, "Fathers,[a] do not exasperate your children; instead, bring them up in the training and instruction of the Lord." Then it says in Colossians 3:21, "Fathers,[a] do not embitter your children, or they will become discouraged." Is it possible to achieve obedience while at the same time cause exasperation, embitterment, and discouragement? Yes, it is! Some examples might be it's time for dinner and Mom calls out, "Turn off the TV right now and come to the table." The show is at a climax and the child is so excited to see the ending, but Mom said, "Right now!" The child can either obey and miss out or disobey and watch the show. This example shows how the two areas can oppose each other. Another is Dad asks his son to help with the grass whereas earlier that day, Mom asked him to help with the laundry. How is the son supposed to obey both parents at once? Again, we can see how we can get out of balance. There are two solutions to these types of conflicts. For the first situation, give time to transition. Say instead, "We're going to eat dinner in five minutes. Find a good stopping place, then come to the table." This gives the child time to watch those last few minutes and come to the table on time. For the second example, use the appeal process.

> Parent: Please do this (cut the grass).
> Child: May I appeal? (Tip: Sometimes, child won't bring any information. They are gaming you. To get them back on track, discontinue appeal until they're ready, i.e., they just have to do what's told. Once they figure out appeal helps them, then continue.)
> Parent: Yes, what is the new information?
> Child: Gives new information (Mom asked me to help with the laundry).
> Parent: Decides (Okay, go ahead and help with laundry). Tip: Check with Mom.
> Child: Follows parent's decisions.

These are two ways to expect obedience yet do it without causing exasperation, embitterment, and discouragement and still stay on the tightrope. The next balancing act is in Proverbs 13:24, "Whoever spares the rod hates their children, but the one who loves their children is careful to discipline them." Verses Romans 1:7 says, "To all in Rome who are loved by God and called to be his holy people: Grace and peace to you from God our Father and from the Lord Jesus Christ." So the next tightrope act is discipline versus grace and peace. The goal: improve behavior without destroying relationships. Below are a list of tips and techniques to consider:

- Discipline defiant disobedience and not mistakes
- First time, give lighter discipline and increase if behavior persists
- Sometimes, grace has more impact than discipline
- Forgive and forget
- Discipline without anger
- Don't discipline a natural consequence. A natural consequence is when nature provides the discipline. For example, you tell your son not to run and he does and falls down and skins his knee. The natural consequence is the pain of the skinned knee. The son will remember not to run so fast or to be more careful next time. There is no need for another consequence or discipline.

By doing these things, you can be balanced in grace, peace, and discipline.

JOSEPH GIAMMARCO

Next Step: Reflection, Application, and Action

Not at all (0) — Slightly (2) — Some (4) — Much (6) — Very Much (8) — Perfect =Jesus (10)

Ask God to reveal where you are, what to do next, and to help you (five or below should take action).

Priority	Basic Question	Statement	Rating	Action to Improve	New Rating	Difference in Rating
Third: Children	Am I balanced between obedience and anger, frustration and discouragement?	I use the appeal process.				
		Give time to transition to obey.				
	Am I balanced between discipline and grace and peace?	I discipline defiant disobedience and not mistakes.				
		First time, I give lighter discipline and increase if persists.				
		Sometimes, I show grace instead of discipline because it has more impact.				
		I forgive and forget.				
		I discipline without anger.				
		I don't discipline natural consequences.				

CHAPTER 20

LOVE YOUR CHILDREN

Love Your Children

No catchy chapter title since this chapter focuses on the same area as "Paul, This Is Your Life." The difference is you'll be measuring where you are in loving your children. Love your children for who they are and not what they do. This is unconditional love. To reinforce this, which would you rather hear if you asked your parents why they loved you: "because you're my child" or "because you are good at sports, school, etc." I think all of us would choose "because you're my child." Do the exercise on the next pages for each child and keep in mind the points below:

- Just as God loves us regardless of our sins, accomplishments, etc. We should love our children because they are worthy of our love because of who they are and not what they do.
- We are human beings, not human doings.
- Don't use activities as a way to accomplish your goals through your children.

Next Step: Reflection, Application, and Action

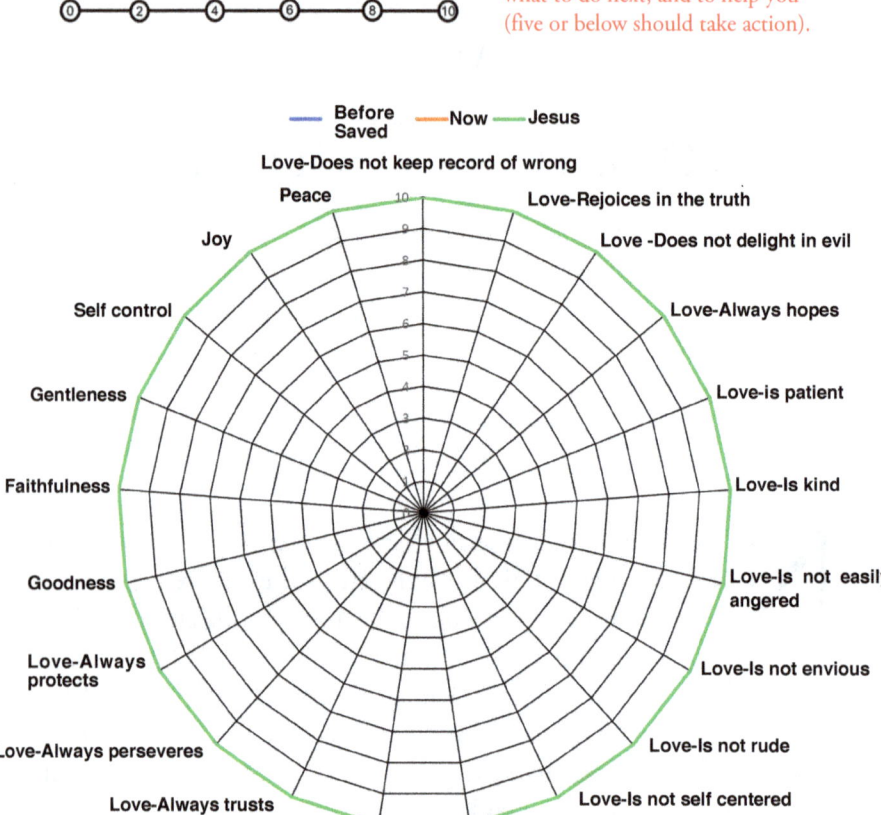

Ask God to reveal where you are, what to do next, and to help you (five or below should take action).

Attributes of Jesus He wants us to have	Definition
Love: Does not keep record of wrong	Forgives and forgets. Overlooks most offenses.
Love: Rejoices in the truth	Celebrates or feels good or encourages others obeying Jesus (the truth).
Love: Does not delight in evil	Does not celebrate or feel good when something bad happens to others or they sin.

GOD'S MESSAGE TO MEN

Attributes of Jesus He wants us to have	Definition
Love: Always hopes	Always has an expectation and desire for good things to happen to others.
Love: Is patient	Able to accept or tolerate delays, problems, or suffering without becoming annoyed or anxious.
Love: Is kind	Having or showing a friendly, generous, and considerate nature.
Love: Is not easily angered	Does not have a quick temper.
Love: Is not envious	Is not jealous, covetous, and resentful.
Love: Is not rude	Is not offensively impolite or ill-mannered.
Love: Is not self-centered	Is not preoccupied with oneself and one's affairs.
Love: Is not boastful	Is not showing excessive pride and self-satisfaction in one's achievements, possessions, or abilities.
Love: Is not proud	Is not having or showing a high or excessively high opinion of oneself or one's importance.
Love: Always trusts	Always has firm belief in the reliability, truth, ability, or strength of others.
Love: Always perseveres	Always continue in a course of action even in the face of difficulty or with little or no prospect of success.
Love: Always protects	Always keep others safe from harm or injury.
Goodness	What we do and say are good and right.
Faithfulness	Trust and loyal on Christ for salvation, believe in the truth/promises of God, and actions match these beliefs.
Gentleness	Humility and thankfulness toward God, and polite, restrained behavior toward others.
Self-control	Choosing to give up trying to control things on our own, surrendering to God for help.
Joy	Choosing to respond to life's difficult situations with inner contentment and satisfaction.
Peace	A state of rest, completeness, or wholeness and not worry because you see things as God sees them.

Next Step: Reflection, Application, and Action

Rating scale: 0 Not at all — 2 Slightly — 4 Some — 6 Much — 8 Very Much — 10 Perfect =Jesus

Ask God to reveal where you are, what to do next, and to help you (five or below should take action).

Priority	Basic Question	Statement	Definition/Detail	Rating	Action to Improve	New Rating	Difference in Rating
Third: Children	Do I love my children unconditionally?	I love my children for who they are versus what they do.					
		I don't use their activities as a way to accomplish my goals or build a monument to me					
		Love: Does not keep record of wrong	Forgives and forgets. Overlooks most offenses.				
		Love: Rejoices in the truth	Celebrates or feels good or encourages others obeying Jesus (the truth).				
		Love: Does not delight in evil	Does not celebrate or feel good when something bad happens to others or they sin.				

GOD'S MESSAGE TO MEN

Priority	Basic Question	Statement	Definition/ Detail	Rating	Action to Improve	New Rating	Difference in Rating
		Love: Always hopes	Always has an expectation and desire for good things to happen to others.				
		Love: Is patient	Able to accept or tolerate delays, problems, or suffering without becoming annoyed or anxious.				
		Love: Is kind	Having or showing a friendly, generous, and considerate nature.				
		Love: Is not easily angered	Does not have a quick temper.				
		Love: Is not envious	Is not jealous, covetous, and resentful.				
		Love: Is not rude	Is not offensively impolite or ill-mannered.				
		Love: Is not self-centered	Is not preoccupied with oneself and one's affairs.				

Priority	Basic Question	Statement	Definition/Detail	Rating	Action to Improve	New Rating	Difference in Rating
		Love: Is not boastful	Is not showing excessive pride and self-satisfaction in one's achievements, possessions, or abilities.				
		Love: Is not proud	Is not having or showing a high or excessively high opinion of oneself or one's importance.				
		Love: Always trusts	Always has firm belief in the reliability, truth, ability, or strength of others.				
		Love: Always perseveres	Always continue in a course of action even in the face of difficulty or with little or no prospect of success.				
		Love: Always protects	Always keep others safe from harm or injury.				

CHAPTER 21

Love Languages for Children

Once again, no fancy title. Love Languages is a concept developed by Gary Chapman. The theory is people have a love language they prefer spoken or acted on by others. When this happens, the person feels loved and appreciated. These words or actions are spontaneous. The goal is by speaking the love language, you keep that person's love tank full. These are the love languages and their definitions:

1. Words of affirmation: Saying supportive things to someone.
2. Acts of service: Doing helpful things for someone.
3. Receiving gifts: Giving gifts to someone that tell them you were thinking about them.
4. Quality time: Spending meaningful time with someone.
5. Physical touch: Being close to and touch someone.

Where families get into trouble is when they're speaking a different language. Usually their own. For example, the dad is cleaning the kitchen because his love language is acts of service meanwhile the daughter is sitting on the couch waiting to talk to her dad and share their day with each other because her gift is quality time. She's mad because he won't talk to her and he's mad because she won't help him. The smart dad would drop what he's doing and go share with his daughter. Next step is for you to go to the Love Language website in the link below and find out you and your children's love language and start speaking theirs to them.

LINK: http://www.5lovelanguages.com/quizzes/child-quiz/
https://www.5lovelanguages.com/quizzes/teen-quiz/

Next Step: Reflection, Application, and Action

Not at all (0) — Slightly (2) — Some (4) — Much (6) — Very Much (8) — Perfect =Jesus (10)

Ask God to reveal where you are, what to do next and to help you (5 or below should take action)

Priority	Basic Question	Statement	Rating	Action to Improve	New Rating	Difference in Rating
Third: Children	Do you know and speak your children's love language?	Understand your children's love language and speak it to them.				

CHAPTER 22

AGES AND STAGES

This chapter is titled "Ages and Stages." The reason for the title is we are going to get into how parents need to transition their parenting style as the child grows. In the end, one of the goals of parenting is to produce adult children who are able to take care of themselves independent of the parents. In the illustration below is an image of a small child, child, teenager, and young adult. The ages are approximate. What is most important is to recognize there are different stages and parents need to change their game as the child matures

Transition from Baby to Adult

Monitoring
- You give advice and monitor.
- They are likely able, but insecure or unwilling.

Empowerment
- You give advice only when asked.
- They are likely able, confident, and willing.

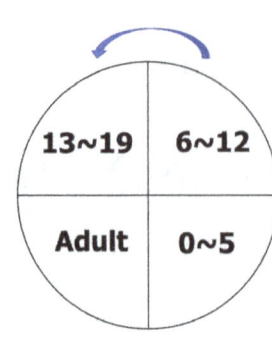

Coach
- You tell, show, and encourage.
- They may be unable, but confident or willing.

Hand Holding
- You tell, show, and do.
- They are likely unable, insecure, or unwilling.

Change your parenting style as the child grows.

Next Step: Reflection, Application, and Action

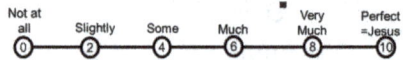

Ask God to reveal where you are, what to do next, and to help you (five or below should take action).

Priority	Basic Question	Statement	Rating	Action to Improve	New Rating	Difference in Rating
Third: Children	I change my parenting style as my children grow.	I				

CHAPTER 23

Offensive Line

This chapter is titled "Offensive Line." The reason for the title is in football, the offensive line is charged with keeping the defense from getting behind the offensive line and get the ball from the quarterback or running back. Children tend to pit one parent against another to get behind the parent's defense and get what they want. To prevent that, parents need to have a unified front. Two techniques to have a unified front is to use the appeal process and practice oneness in communication. In the end, both parents agree on the direction and give to the children. Remember you're the parents and it's your right to decide what the direction is for the child. Do these two things, and you will keep the child out of the backfield, and you will have a unified front so the children will not divide and conquer you. See the illustration below for an image of this process.

JOSEPH GIAMMARCO

Unified Parenting

Warning: Children tend to pit one parent against the other, so…

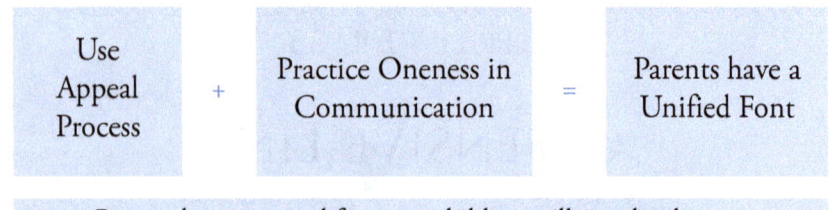

Parents have a united front, so children will not divide you.

Next Step: Reflection, Application, and Action

Not at all — Slightly — Some — Much — Very Much — Perfect =Jesus
0 — 2 — 4 — 6 — 8 — 10

Ask God to reveal where you are, what to do next, and to help you (five or below should take action).

Priority	Basic Question	Statement	Rating	Action to Improve	New Rating	Difference in Rating
	As parents, we have a united front, so our children will not divide us.	We use the appeal process.				
		We practice oneness in communication.				

CHAPTER 24

Trash Van

This chapter is titled "Trash Van." The meaning behind the title is that so many families spend so much time in their vans rushing around to different activities, stopping for fast food, eating in the car, etc., the van becomes one big trash can. Thus, trash van! Many families operate at a frantic, overwhelming pace because the parents want to expose their children to as many things and people as possible to teach them life skills. The description of this lifestyle is something like this:

1. Kids are involved in several extracurricular activities.
2. Parents are rushing around driving to practices/games/meetings.
3. Meals are fast food and in the car.
4. Homework done in the car.
5. Kids and parents not getting enough sleep.
6. The house is a wreck.
7. The car is a trash can.
8. Everyone is stressed.

Below is the negative by-product of this lifestyle:

1. Stop paying attention to God.
2. Relinquish your duty to teach your children yourself to others.
3. Give time with your children to others.
4. Reduce time for husband and wife to date.
5. Become a children (activity)-centered family.
6. Increased discipline issues (everyone tired and cranky).
7. Increase chances you are showing them you love them for what they do.
8. Increase chances to use kids' activities to build monuments to parents.
9. Sabbath is full of activities and things not done the first six days.
10. Spending more than budget.
11. More sickness.
12. Begin to covet other children (superstars).
13. Grades drop.
14. Children get burnout and want to quit.

You can achieve the same result with a calm, easy pace. The description of this lifestyle is something like this:

1. Kids are involved in at most one extracurricular activities only for right reason, i.e., I don't like soccer, but my best friend is playing so I want to. It's better to get them together sometimes.
2. Parents teach life skills by having kids help with activities at home.
3. Eat home-cooked meals together.
4. Homework done at home at a reasonable time.
5. Kids and parents getting enough sleep.
6. The house is orderly.
7. The car is clean.
8. Everyone is relaxed.

GOD'S MESSAGE TO MEN

The positive by-product of this lifestyle is the following:

1. God as first priority.
2. Teach your children life skills yourself.
3. Have more quality and quantity time.
4. Increase husband and wife dating.
5. Become a marriage-centered family.
6. Reduce discipline issues (everyone well rested and calm).
7. Decrease chances you are showing them you love them for what they do.
8. Decrease chances to use kids' activities to build monuments to parents.
9. Relax on the Sabbath.
10. Spending within budget.
11. Less sickness.
12. Lessen chances to covet other children (superstars).
13. Good grades.
14. Children not quitting.

Strive for family life to be calm and easy paced.

Next Step: Reflection, Application, and Action

Not at all (0) — Slightly (2) — Some (4) — Much (6) — Very Much (8) — Perfect =Jesus (10)

Ask God to reveal where you are, what to do next, and to help you (five or below should take action).

Priority	Basic Question	Statement	Rating	Action to Improve	New Rating	Difference in Rating
Third: Children	Our family life is a calm and easy paced.	The house is orderly.				
		Car is clean.				
		Everyone is relaxed.				

CHAPTER 25

NOT A SUGGESTION AND NOT JUST FOR KIDS

I chose this title "Not a Suggestion and Not Just for Kids" because in this chapter, we are going to talk about an area sometimes misunderstood as a wish from God to our kids. As parents, we often remind our children of this, but we never think how it applies to us adults. It's the Fifth Commandment and is written at the top of the second tablet God wrote the five commandments written related to people. The first tablet contains five commandments related to God. See the illustration below:

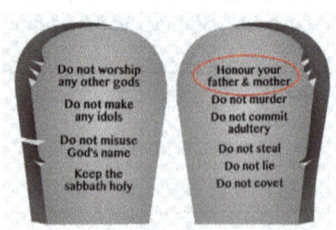

Written in Stone
Commandment
Related to People

It's "Honor your father and mother." And the verse that applies it is Exodus 20:12, "Honor your father and your mother, so that you may live long in the land the Lord your God is giving you." You notice it is a commandment and not suggestion, hope, or wish. You'll also notice there is no age limit or ceiling on who this applies to. It's also a commandment with a promise. If you obey it, you will live out all the days God has granted you. And those days will be quality ones. The next two verses reinforce Exodus 20:12. Matthew 15:1–6 says, "Then some Pharisees and teachers of the law came to Jesus from Jerusalem and asked, 'Why do your disciples break the tradition of the elders? They don't wash their hands before they eat!' Jesus replied, 'And why do you break the command of God for the sake of your tradition? For God said, "Honor your father and mother"[a] and "Anyone who curses their father or mother is to be put to death."[b] But you say that if anyone declares that what might have been used to help their father or mother is devoted to God, they are not to honor their father or mother with it. Thus you nullify the word of God for the sake of your tradition.'" Jesus is talking to adults and telling them not to break the commandments. Here are some verses from Proverbs 10:1, 15:20, 17:25, 19:26, and 20:20, which boils down to either we can bring joy or grief to our parents.

Here are some challenging questions to ask yourself:

- Is your life honoring to your parents? In other words, are you doing right in the eyes of the Lord?
- Are you helping your parents?
- Do you prize/revere your parents?
- How's your relationship with your parents?
- Are you harboring unforgiveness/need to ask for forgiveness?
    Mark 11:25 says, "And when you stand praying, if you hold anything against anyone, forgive them, so that your Father in heaven may forgive you your sins," and Matthew 5:24 says, "Leave your gift there in front of the altar. First go and be reconciled to them; then come and offer your gift."

- Are you repeating the bad/good ways your parents did to your children?

God expects even as adults, we need to honor our parents regardless of our upbringing.

Next Step: Reflection, Application, and Action

Not at all (0) — Slightly (2) — Some (4) — Much (6) — Very Much (8) — Perfect =Jesus (10)

Ask God to reveal where you are, what to do next, and to help you (five or below should take action).

Priority	Basic Question	Statement	Rating	Action to Improve	New Rating	Difference in Rating
Third: Children	As an adult, do I honor my father and mother?	I help my parents.				
		I prize and revere my parents.				
		I have a good relationship with my parents.				
		I'm not harboring unforgiveness or needing to ask my parents for forgiveness.				
		I repeat the good things and not the bad things to my children.				

SECTION 4

Fourth Priority Is World

CHAPTER 26

Mad Cow

This is the first chapter in the World Section as our fourth priority relationship behind God, wife, and children. I chose this title "Mad Cow" after mad cow disease. Mad cow disease, also called Creutzfeldt-Jakob Disease (CJD), is a fatal disease that slowly destroys the brain and spinal cord in cattle. People cannot get mad cow disease. However, in rare cases, they can get a human form of mad cow disease called variant Creutzfeldt-Jakob disease, which is also fatal. In this chapter, we are going to study whose things is it anyway and for whose glory is everything. We are going to study King Nebuchadnezzar. According to Wikipedia, King Nebuchadnezzar is known to modern historians as Nebuchadnezzar II. He ruled Babylonia from 605 to 562 BC. As the most influential and longest-reigning kings of the Neo-Babylonian period, Nebuchadnezzar conducted the city of Babylon to its height of power and prosperity. This king was very successful at building the Babylonian Empire and was very proud of his accomplishments. Let's find out what happens to someone with this pride. It says in Daniel 4:1–37, "[a]King Nebuchadnezzar, To the nations and peoples of every language, who live in all the earth: May you prosper greatly! It is my pleasure to tell you about the miraculous signs and wonders that the Most High God has performed for me. How great are his signs, how mighty his wonders! His kingdom is an eternal kingdom; his dominion endures from generation to generation. I, Nebuchadnezzar, was at home in my palace, contented and prosperous. I had a dream that made me afraid. As I was lying in bed, the images and visions that passed through my mind terrified me. So I commanded that all the wise men of Babylon be brought before me to interpret the dream for me. When the magicians, enchanters, astrologers[b] and diviners came, I told them the dream, but they could not interpret it for me. Finally, Daniel came into my presence and I told him the dream. (He is called Belteshazzar, after the name of my god, and the spirit of the holy gods is in him.) I said, 'Belteshazzar, chief of the magicians, I know that the spirit of the holy gods is in you, and no mystery is too difficult for you. Here is my dream; interpret it for me. These are the visions I saw while lying in bed: I looked, and there before me stood a tree in the middle of the land. Its height was enormous. The tree grew large and strong and its top touched the sky; it was visible to the ends of the earth. Its leaves were beautiful, its fruit abundant, and on it was food for all. Under it the wild animals found shelter, and the birds lived in its branches; from it every creature was fed. In the visions I saw while lying in bed, I looked, and there before me was a holy one, a messenger,[c] coming down from heaven. He called in a loud voice: "Cut down the tree and trim off its branches; strip off its leaves and scatter its fruit. Let the animals flee from under it and the birds from its branches. But let the stump and its roots, bound with iron and bronze, remain in the ground, in the grass of the field. Let him be drenched with the dew of heaven, and let him live with the animals among the plants of the earth. Let his mind be changed from that of a man and let him be given the mind of an animal, till seven times[d] pass by for him. 17 The decision is announced by messengers, the holy ones declare the verdict, so that the living may know that the Most High is sovereign over all kingdoms on earth and gives them to anyone he wishes and sets over them the lowliest of people." This is the dream that I, King Nebuchadnezzar, had. Now, Belteshazzar, tell me what it means, for none of the wise men in my kingdom can interpret it for me. But you can, because the spirit of the holy gods is in you.' Then Daniel (also called Belteshazzar) was greatly perplexed for a time, and his thoughts terrified him. So the king said, 'Belteshazzar, do not let the dream or its meaning alarm you.' Belteshazzar answered, 'My lord, if only the dream applied to your enemies and its meaning to your adversaries! The tree you saw, which grew large and strong, with its top touching the sky, visible to the whole earth, with beautiful leaves and abundant fruit, providing food for all, giving shelter to the wild animals, and having nesting places in its branches for the birds—Your Majesty, you are that tree! You have become great and strong; your greatness has grown until it reaches the sky, and your dominion extends to distant parts of the earth. Your Majesty saw a holy one, a messenger, coming down from heaven and saying, "Cut down the tree and destroy it, but leave the stump, bound with iron and bronze, in the grass of the field, while its roots remain in the ground. Let him be drenched with the dew of heaven; let him live with the wild animals, until seven times pass by for him." This is the interpretation, Your Majesty, and this is the decree the Most High has issued against my lord the king: You will be driven away from people and will live with the wild animals; you will eat grass like the ox and be drenched with the dew of heaven. Seven times will pass by for you until you acknowledge that the Most High is sovereign over all kingdoms on earth and gives them to anyone he wishes. The command to leave the stump of the tree with its roots means that your kingdom will be restored to you when you acknowledge that Heaven rules. Therefore, Your Majesty, be pleased to accept my advice: Renounce your sins by doing what is right, and your wickedness by being kind to the oppressed. It may be that then your prosperity will continue.' All this happened to King Nebuchadnezzar. Twelve months later, as the king was walking on the roof of the royal palace of Babylon, he said, 'Is not this the great Babylon I have built as the royal residence, by my mighty power and for the glory of my majesty?' Even as the words were on his lips, a voice came from heaven, 'This is what is decreed for you, King Nebuchadnezzar: Your royal authority has been taken from you. You will be driven away from people and will live with the wild animals; you will eat grass like the ox. Seven times will pass by for you until you acknowledge that the Most High is sovereign over all kingdoms on earth and gives them to anyone he wishes.' Immediately what had been said about Nebuchadnezzar was fulfilled. He was driven away from people and ate grass like the ox. His body was drenched with the dew of heaven until his hair grew like the feathers of an eagle and his nails like the claws of a bird. At the end of that time, I, Nebuchadnezzar, raised my eyes toward heaven, and my sanity was restored. Then I praised the Most High; I honored and glorified him who lives forever. His dominion is an eternal dominion; his kingdom endures from generation to generation. All the peoples of the earth are regarded as nothing. He does as he pleases with the powers of heaven and the peoples of the earth. No one can hold back his hand or say to him: 'What have you done?' At the same time that my sanity was restored, my honor and splendor were returned to me for the glory of my kingdom. My advisers and nobles sought me out, and I was restored to my throne and became even greater than before. Now I, Nebuchadnezzar, praise and exalt and glorify the King of heaven, because everything he does is right and all his ways are just. And those who walk in pride he is able to humble."

In short, because King Nebuchadnezzar believed all he had accomplished was by him and for him, he was driven from his throne and lived as a wild animal (mad cow) seven years until he acknowledged that everything belongs to God for His glory.

What can we learn:

>Realize all you have belongs to God for His glory and he allows us to manage it.
>*Use your time, talents, money, possessions to glorify God.*
>Finally, to avoid becoming a mad cow, realize God owns it all!

GOD'S MESSAGE TO MEN

Next Step: Reflection, Application, and Action

Not at all — 0
Slightly — 2
Some — 4
Much — 6
Very Much — 8
Perfect =Jesus — 10

Ask God to reveal where you are, what to do next, and to help you (five or below should take action).

Priority	Basic Question	Statement	Rating	Action to Improve	New Rating	Difference in Rating
Fourth: World	I realize God owns it all.					

CHAPTER 27

How Now Brown Cow

Now that we've learned God owns it all and it's our job to manage it for him, we come to our next chapter titled "How Now Brown Cow" This is a phrase used in teaching to demonstrate rounded vowel sounds. Each "ow" sound in the phrase represents the diphthong/aʊ/. The use of the phrase "how now brown cow" in teaching can be traced back to at least 1926. In this chapter titled "How Now Brown Cow," we will be talking about "how to" tips in managing God's world. Plus, we have the Bible verse Psalm 50:10, "For every animal of the forest is mine, and the cattle on a thousand hills." This is God speaking about how he owns it all. Mix it all together, and poof, out comes the title How now brown cow. We are going to talk about time, talent, money, and possessions.

Time

- Remember the Sabbath and keep it holy. Six days you shall work, and on the seventh, rest.
- Plan to do all your work in six days (that includes housework, school work, yard work, etc.). Spend the seventh to unplug. Reflect on God, and enjoy the relationships He's blessed you with.

- If you're not able to do this at first, maybe you need to prioritize your time more effectively.

Talents

- Ask God to reveal your SHAPES and how to use it to glorify Him thru making/teaching disciples.
- S:Spiritual gifts, H: Heart or passion, A: Abilities, P: Personality, E: Experiences, S: Sphere of influence or position

See the example in the next illustration. There are links that bring you to sites to help you fill out various sections.

Make sure you are even in the right ministry and have one (SHAPES): Joe's Example

Categories	Spiritual Gifts	Heart or Passion	Abilities	Personality	Experiences	Sphere of influence or placement
Instructions	Go to following website and take Spiritual Gift Survey https://www.biblesprout.com/articles/god/holy-spirit/spiritual-gifts-test/. Also think about times people have said, "Wow, that was incredible!" These will give you indication of your Spiritual Gifts too. Trial and error can help as well. List results below.	What things or people are you passionate about? What things do you think or dream about helping when you have time? What things make you angry in a way to make positive action? After thinking, put your answer in the Results section	What unique abilities do you have which are natural and learned (school, job, hobbies, etc.)? After thinking about this, write down in the Results box below.	Go to link and find out your love language and list top one in the Results Row below http://www.5lovelanguages.com/quizzes/singles-quiz/. Fill out the Personality Profile by searching the internet for OSPP Four Temperaments Tests and write down the in the Results box below.	Think about triumphs, tragedies, unique situations you been in or through. List them in the Results box below.	Think about the unique sphere of influence or placement which you have in your family, community, church, work, city, state, country, world, people groups, etc. Remember when we hear the great commission we think about physical distance, but demographic distances are also important. List these in the Results box below.

Categories	Spiritual Gifts	Heart or Passion	Abilities	Personality	Experiences	Sphere of influence or placement
Results	My Primary Gifts Teaching (84%) Knowledge (78%) Administration (75%)	-Helping men have a stronger relationship to God -Helping Christian organizations (ministries, churches and companies) be more effective -Help prisoners break the cycle of crime	Engineer, quality, management, project management, problem solving, teaching, Stand-up comedy, fishing, speak three languages, like to teach own material, like to start new things (bored maintaining)	Love Language: Words of Affirmation Main Personality: Melancholy (Perfect) Secondary Personality: Choleric (Powerful)	Italian American, raised by immigrants who were grandparent age. Born again. Divorced. Two children don't speak with. Trips: Ukraine, Haiti	Christian business owners and African Americans
My unique ministry to build God's kingdom (ideas)	Communicate and encourage through teaching (live, YouTube, Zoom, books, etc.) how men can have a stronger relationship to God, Christian ministries and businesses can be more effective in building God's kingdom. Transplant Texas PEP (Prisoner Entrepreneur Program) to Ohio and beyond.					

Categories	Spiritual Gifts	Heart or Passion	Abilities	Personality	Experiences	Sphere of influence or placement
God's command to His followers	"Then Jesus came to them and said, 'All authority in heaven and on earth has been given to me. Therefore go and make disciples of all nations, baptizing them in the name of the Father and of the Son and of the Holy Spirit, and teaching them to obey everything I have commanded you. And surely I am with you always, to the very end of the age." (Matthew 28:18–20)		"On one occasion, while he was eating with them, he gave them this command: 'Do not leave Jerusalem, but wait for the gift my Father promised, which you have heard me speak about. For John Baptized with water, but in a few days you will be baptized with the Holy Spirit.' Then they gathered around him and asked them, 'Lord, are you at this time going to restore the kingdom to Israel?' He said to them: 'It is not for you to know the times and or dates the Father has set by his own authority, But you will receive power when the Holy Spirit comes one you; and you will be my witnesses in Jerusalem, and in all Judea and Samaria, and to the ends of the earth.' After he said this, he was taken up before there very eyes, and a cloud his him from there sight." (Acts 1:4–9)		Build my kingdom: 1) Invite others to join. 2) After they join, teach them the way to live. Jesus asks: Who knows me because of you? Who is like me because of you?
The ultimate goal	To love God by obeying His commandments.					
The motive	God is worthy of our love.					

Money

- Tithe: Give your first and best 10 percent as a minimum to be used to glorify God.
- If you're not able to do this at first, ask God to give you the faith to work toward this.
- We have a family budget which is agreed to by the husband and wife and one of the two keep track of it to adjust as needed. Ideally, you're within your budget and your budget is within your income.
- Look for opportunities to be a better steward of what you're given (needs vs. wants).

Possessions

- Recognize what you have is God's. Take good care of them (material possessions, health, etc.).
- God gave these to provide for your needs and the needs of others. Look for ways to use for this purpose.
- Get rid of stuff that gets in the way of glorifying God, serving others, and enjoying the relationships God has blessed you with.
- Be content with what you have and not covet other people's possessions (Tenth Commandment).

So to use what you are given by God to glorify Him and being a good steward of what God has given you will prevent you from being a mad cow and instead be a how now brown cow.

JOSEPH GIAMMARCO

Next Step: Reflection, Application, and Action

Not at all (0) — Slightly (2) — Some (4) — Much (6) — Very Much (8) — Perfect =Jesus (10)

Ask God to reveal where you are, what to do next, and to help you (five or below should take action).

Priority	Basic Question	Statement	Definition/ Detail	Rating	Action to Improve	New Rating	Difference in Rating
World: Fourth Priority	I remember the Sabbath and keep it holy.	On the seventh day, I unplug from my usual work.					
		On the seventh day, I reflect on God.					
		On the seventh day, I enjoy the relationships he's blessed me with.					
	I understand my SHAPES.	I've done the SHAPES exercise and understand the ministry God has for me.					
		I'm involved in the ministry I've learned from doing SHAPES.					
	I tithe 10 percent of my income?						
	Family budget?	We have one.					
		Both husband and wife agree to it.	Use oneness of communication.				
		One of the two keep track of it.					
		It is within the income.					
		Adjustments are being made to stay on track.					

GOD'S MESSAGE TO MEN

Priority	Basic Question	Statement	Definition/ Detail	Rating	Action to Improve	New Rating	Difference in Rating
	Possessions?	We take good care of them (material possessions, health, etc.).					
		We use these to provide for your needs and the needs of others.					
		We get rid of stuff that gets in the way of glorifying God, serving others, and enjoying the relationships God has blessed us with.					
		We are content with what we have and not covet other people's possessions (Tenth Commandment).					

CHAPTER 28

PEACE AND VICTORY

This next chapter is titled the promise of "Peace and Victory." I named it that way because we're going to talk about peace and victory. Not only is peace and victory possible, but it's probable. It can be attainable. I want to give you a little background about myself. I became a believer when I was eighteen years old. I'm now sixty-one years old. That's forty-three years ago if I've done my math right. Even though I've been a Christian a long time, I find myself repeating the same sins over and over like I was never saved. Some areas of my life got worse. So God had to teach me something recently. I'm not there yet, but I wanted to share with you and hopefully you can learn from them as well. Some dear people helped me and the Lord helped me to see as well. I'm not going to mention their names here because they're not ones seeking credit, but I'm very grateful. One of the things they challenged is why do we keep doing the same old sin over and over, yet we keep asking for forgiveness. Then we sin over and over again. I think we've all been there. They pointed out Romans 6: "What shall we say, then? Shall we go on sinning so that grace may increase? By no means! We are those who have died to sin; how can we live in it any longer? Or don't you know that all of us who were baptized into Christ Jesus were baptized into his death? We were therefore buried with him through baptism into death so that, just as Christ was raised from the dead through the glory of the Father, we too may live a new life. For if we have been united with him in a death like his, we will certainly also be united with him in a resurrection like his. For we know that our old self was crucified with him so that the body ruled by sin might be done away with, that we should no longer be slaves to sin—because anyone who has died has been set free from sin. Now if we died with Christ, we believe that we will also live with him. For we know that since Christ was raised from the dead, he cannot die again; death no longer has mastery over him. The death he died, he died to sin once for all; but the life he lives, he lives to God. In the same way, count yourselves dead to sin but alive to God in Christ Jesus. Therefore do not let sin reign in your mortal body so that you obey its evil desires. Do not offer any part of yourself to sin as an instrument of wickedness, but rather offer yourselves to God as those who have been brought from death to life; and offer every part of yourself to him as an instrument of righteousness. For sin shall no longer be your master, because you are not under the law, but under grace.

"What then? Shall we sin because we are not under the law but under grace? By no means! Don't you know that when you offer yourselves to someone as obedient slaves, you are slaves of the one you obey—whether you are slaves to sin, which leads to death, or to obedience, which leads to righteousness? But thanks be to God that, though you used to be slaves to sin, you have come to obey from your heart the pattern of teaching that has now claimed your allegiance. You have been set free from sin and have become slaves to righteousness.

"I am using an example from everyday life because of your human limitations. Just as you used to offer yourselves as slaves to impurity and to ever-increasing wickedness, so now offer yourselves as slaves to righteousness leading to holiness. When you were slaves to sin, you were free from the control of righteousness. What benefit did you reap at that time from the things you are now ashamed of? Those things result in death! But now that you have been set free from sin and have become slaves of God, the benefit you reap leads to holiness, and the result is eternal life. For the wages of sin is death, but the gift of God is eternal life in Christ Jesus our Lord."

This chapter basically says, "The old man is dead and we're set free from sin." If that's true, then why do I keep sinning? My answers before were "I'm a sinner and that's my nature so there is nothing I can do about it" or "the Devil made me do it." Romans 6 taught me I have a choice to leave the old man dead and be set free from sin. Another thing I've dealt with in my life is fear, worry, and anxiety. I learned the opposite is faith. I wasn't doing things with faith, but under my own control. The less control we give God, the worse it gets. In Philippians 4:6–7, it says, "Do not be anxious about anything, but in every situation, by prayer and petition, with thanksgiving, present your requests to God. And the peace of God, which transcends all understanding, will guard your hearts and your minds in Christ Jesus." I started to realize I spent most of my life not in peace, yet you hear throughout the Bible peace. The world's definition is everything is under control and good. Jesus and the Bible never explain it that way. Jesus says, "In this world, you will have trouble, but be of good cheer. I have overcome the world, peace I leave you, peace I give you, and let your heart not be troubled and be not afraid."

We see when Jesus was in the boat sleeping; meanwhile, his disciples were afraid of the storm. The disciples reacted just like the world. Things aren't going well; why are you sleeping? Jesus asleep in the boat is a symbol of what peace is. We're going to have storms. Nothing is promised to us. We're not going to have everything good all the time. We don't live in a Facebook world where everything it good. Look at the patriarchs; no one would ever look at their Facebook. Abraham, the man of faith, took matters in his own hands and had Ishmael. Twice, he asked his wife to say she was his sister to avoid being killed. Moses, who was lavished with tons of praise after he died, was a murderer. He refused to help God and got angry a lot which kept him from entering the promised land. Yet God said no one knew God like Moses did. David, a man after God's own heart, was a murderer, adulterer, family was out of control. Son raped a sister, brother killed that brother, and son tried to kill the king. These guys had real trouble. We would never read their Facebook.

The last thing I'm going to explain another way to win the battle of peace and victory. The armor of God. Ephesians 6:10–19 says, "Finally, be strong in the Lord and in his mighty power. Put on the full armor of God so that you can take your stand against the devil's schemes. For our struggle is not against flesh and blood, but against the rulers, against the authorities, against the powers of this dark world and against the spiritual forces of evil in the heavenly realms. Therefore put on the full armor of God, so that when the day of evil comes, you may be able to stand your ground, and after you have done everything, to stand. Stand firm then, with the belt of truth buckled around your waist, with the breastplate of righteousness in place, and with your feet fitted with the readiness that comes from the gospel of peace. In addition to all this, take up the shield of faith, with which you can extinguish all the flaming arrows of the evil one. Take the helmet of salvation and the sword of the Spirit, which is the word of God. And pray in the Spirit on all occasions with all kinds of prayers and requests. With this in mind, be alert and always keep on praying for all the saints. Pray also for me, that whenever I open my mouth, words may be given me so that I will fearlessly make known the mystery of the gospel, for which I am an ambassador in chains. Pray that I may declare it fearlessly, as I should."

Key points:

- We are in a spiritual battle against Satan and his demons.
- God has designed the armor specially to fight our adversary.
- When we use all the armor, we will be able to stand our ground and be victorious against the evil one.

1. Belt of truth: This is what holds everything is place. The fundamental truth is God is all powerful, always present (everywhere all the time), knows all things (past present and future), perfect in love (and loves you), all good (without sin), creator of all things (holds the universe in His hand), promise maker and keeper (never breaks a promise), and a perfect balance of grace, mercy, and justice. Nothing is too hard for Him! Any problem we are facing is smaller

than our God. When we face problems, we should see that our God is greater than any problem, can overcome all of them, and will fight for you. We need to keep our eyes on Jesus so we don't sink. Satan wants to cast doubt and lie and try to make you think God is not that powerful or interested in your problems or your problem is bigger than God. If we give in to this, it's like being in the battle with our pants down

2. Breastplate of righteousness: This guards our vital organs. Once you're saved, remember the old man is dead and the new one is raised with Christ. Christ no longer condemns us. Our righteousness comes from Christ. We put on the Holy Spirit and are filled and have the mind of Christ. Our sins are forgiven and are as far as the east to the west in God's eyes. Satan wants to accuse you of past sins to make you feel unworthy and unsaved.

3. Feet fitted with the Gospel of peace: As you want to share the gospel and help others as Jesus has commanded you and equipped you, remember you need to be ready/available. Remember the Spirit, by grace, enables people to be saved and not by your own effort. Remembering this will help you to be sure footed. Satan tries to discourage you and put many obstacles and traps in your path from sharing the gospel and helping others. When you do, he wants to make you feel frustrated when people don't respond right away. Never give up

4. Shield of faith: Having faith that what God has promised, He will deliver. Five promises. You are to act as you already have it. Allowing God to defend and fight for us while we watch in peace. We should be like Jesus sleeping in the boat while the storm raged. He wasn't worried because God is bigger than the storm. Cling to God's promises. Satan wants us to believe God is not faithful and won't deliver us. He wants us to panic and take matters into our own hands

5. Helmet of salvation: Ability to discern truth of God from the lies of Satan. Are these thoughts your own? If not, you

can take them captive by telling Satan and his demons to flee in the name of Jesus and by his Blood. Satan wants to plant lies in our mind and play on our emotions so that we act like the buried old man (we dig him up).
6. Sword of the Spirit: This is an offensive and defensive weapon. Knowing God's word and quoting it back to Satan not only defends us against attack, but allows us to advance against our enemy. For example, when Satan tries to make you worry, then recall and quote scripture related to it. Satan can't handle the truth of God's word and flees. He tried to keep us from knowing His word and tries to twist it against us.
7. Prayer: Like communication on the battlefield, prayer helps us let God know what we need and to help us. Satan tries to keep us from praying and discourages us from doing it. Then he can cut us off from God.

Notice there is no armor on the back of the soldier because a good soldier never turns his back on the enemy and retreats. We have a Mighty God, so we should always be advancing and moving forward!

In summary:

1. Choose to leave the dead man buried (Romans 6).
2. Pray for the peace that surpasses understanding (Ephesians 6:10–19).
3. Realize there will be trouble and react with calmness.
4. Put on the full armor of God to fight Satan and his demons.

ABOUT THE AUTHOR

Joe Giammarco was born and raised in Columbus, Ohio. He is a first generation Italian American. His parents immigrated to the United States from Italy after World War II. After high school, he enrolled at the Ohio State University. There he received a bachelor's and master's in mechanical engineering. He worked as an engineer for thirty-seven years, five years at General Motors and the last thirty-two years at Honda. He retired in 2020. In his free time, he especially enjoys fishing. He currently resides in Dublin, Ohio (a suburb of Columbus, Ohio). This is his first book.

www.ingramcontent.com/pod-product-compliance
Lightning Source LLC
Chambersburg PA
CBHW070552160426
43199CB00014B/2474